ALMOST, MAINE

BY JOHN CARIANI

★ Revised Edition

★

DRAMATISTS
PLAY SERVICE
INC.

2

for Northern Maine
and the people who live there

ALMOST, MAINE was produced by Jack Thomas/Bulldog Theatrical and Bruce Payne at the Daryl Roth Theatre, in New York City, opening on January 12, 2006. It was directed by Gabriel Barre; the set design was by James Youmans; the costume design was by Pamela Scofield; the lighting design was by Jeff Croiter; the incidental music was by Julian Fleisher; and the production stage manager was Karyn Meek. The cast was as follows:

PETE, STEVE, LENDALL, RANDY, MAN .... Todd Cerveris
GINETTE, GLORY,
WAITRESS, GAYLE, HOPE .... Finnerty Steeves
EAST, JIMMY, CHAD, PHIL, DAVE .... Justin Hagan
SANDRINE, MARVALYN, MARCI, RHONDA .... Miriam Shor

ALMOST, MAINE received its world premiere production at the Portland Stage Company (Anita Stewart, Artistic Director; Tami Ramaker, Managing Director) in Portland, Maine on October 29, 2004. It was directed by Gabriel Barre; the set design was by James Youmans; the costume design was by Pamela Scofield; the lighting design was by Tim Hunter; the incidental music was by Julian Fleisher; and the production stage manager was Myles C. Hatch. The cast was as follows:

PETE, MAN, LENDALL, RANDY, MAN .... Larry Nathanson
GINETTE, GLORY, GAYLE, HOPE .... Wendy Stetson
EAST, STEVE, CHAD, PHIL, DAVE .... Justin Hagan
WOMAN, MARVALYN, MARCI, RHONDA .... Ibi Janko

ALMOST, MAINE was developed at the Cape Cod Theatre Project (Andy Polk, Artistic Director) in 2002.

PLAYWRIGHT'S NOTES

On the text:

Please read and consider the stage directions carefully. They are a part of the play and many are crucial to telling the story.

On punctuation:

Almost, Maine employs a lot of very specific overlapping dialogue. You'll often see this symbol: //. It will appear inside a particular character's line. It simply means that the next character to speak should begin his/her line where the // appears in the speech of the character who is currently speaking. Sometimes this "railroad tracks" method is hard to work out on the written page, so you will also see this symbol: >. It will appear mid-sentence at the end of a line that is not a complete thought. It simply means that the character speaking should drive through to the end of the thought, which will be continued in his/her character's next line(s).

On place:

Almost, Maine is not a coastal town. It is nowhere near the ocean. And it doesn't exist. It is a mythical composite of several northern Maine towns. Were it to exist, Almost would be located in the remote heart of Aroostook (say, "uh-ROO-stick") County, the sparsely populated, northernmost county in Maine. It would occupy unorganized territory that is officially designated as Township Thirteen, Range Seven, or T13-R7. T13-R7 is some seventy-five miles northwest of the northern terminus of Interstate 95; some two hundred miles northwest of the ocean (at its closest); some three hundred miles north of Portland, ME; and some four hundred miles north of Boston, MA. It is far away from things. (See the map at the back of this volume.)

Winters in Almost, Maine are long, cold, and snowy. It often feels like winter up there from October to May. The area's average January temperature is nine degrees Fahrenheit; average annual snowfall is 115 inches. Winters can also be pretty bleak, because the days are short (less than nine hours at the winter solstice), and the town is in a rolling, empty land of wide open space and big sky.

Potato farms dominate to the east; the expansive North Maine Woods are to the west. *National Geographic* once printed something to this effect: "They call Montana 'Big Sky Country.' Well … 'they' haven't seen Northern Maine."

On the northern lights:

The northern lights are brilliant, ribbon-like, other-worldly displays of light. Northern Mainers are fortunate: They live just inside the southernmost tip of a ring defining the area in which the northern lights regularly appear. Growing up, I remember being treated to a northern lights show at least once a year.

The northern lights occur when atoms become "excited." During solar storms, electrons are sent streaming towards the earth. As these electrons enter the earth's atmosphere, they strike and excite atoms, ionizing them — charging them by knocking out an electron. When this happens to enough atoms, the brilliant light display that is the aurora borealis hovers and streaks across the sky. When the aurora fades, it's because the affected atoms have returned to their grounded state. *Almost, Maine* is a play about people who are normally very grounded, but who have become very excited by love … and other extraordinary occurrences.

On time:

The plot of each scene in *Almost, Maine* climaxes with some sort of "magical moment." I have this notion that the magical moments in all of the scenes are happening at exactly the same time — as the clock strikes nine — and that the northern lights and these magical moments are giving rise to one another. At first, I thought it might be neat to have the northern lights appear as each magical moment occurs. But I didn't want to dilute the climax of each scene or muddle the impact of the magical moments with fancy northern lights displays. So I thought it might be better to revisit the northern lights in the transitions between each scene of the play. These "revisitings" will be denoted as "transitional auroras" in the script and will be suggested throughout. They might help audiences understand that each scene of *Almost, Maine* is taking place at the same time, and that this play is all about one moment in time — what happens to people in a heartbeat.

On the people:

The people of Almost, Maine are not simpletons. They are not hicks or rednecks. They are not quaint, quirky eccentrics. They don't wear funny clothes and funny hats. They don't have funny Maine accents. They are not "Down Easters." They are not fishermen or lobstermen. They don't wear galoshes and rain hats. They don't say, "Ayuh."

The people of Almost, Maine are ordinary people. They work hard for a living. They are extremely dignified. They are honest and true. They are not cynical. They are not sarcastic. They are not glib. But this does not mean that they're dumb. They're very smart. They just take time to wonder about things. They speak simply, honestly, truly, and from the heart. They are never precious about what they say or do.

On presenting *Almost, Maine*:

Please keep in mind that "cute" will kill this play. *Almost, Maine* is inherently pretty sweet. There is no need to sentimentalize the material. Just ... let it be what it is — a play about real people who are really, truly, honestly dealing with the toughest thing there is to deal with in life: love.

If you are involved in a production of *Almost, Maine*, please refer to the notes section in the back of this volume.

CASTING NOTES

Almost, Maine is a play for four actors. In my mind, these actors should be in their late twenties/into their thirties. However, I have seen the play done beautifully by four actors who were in their forties.

Almost, Maine is also a play for as many as nineteen actors.

The actor who plays the MAN in "Story of Hope" should be short or thin.

Program Note: If in your program or playbill you plan to include a table of contents in which you list each scene, the characters in each scene, and the actors playing each character, please list the waitress from "Sad and Glad" as WAITRESS; and please list the man in "Story of Hope" as MAN. Please do not list SUZETTE from "Story of Hope" at all.

SCENE BREAKDOWN

PROLOGUE

ACT ONE
Scene 1: HER HEART
Scene 2: SAD AND GLAD
Scene 3: THIS HURTS
Scene 4: GETTING IT BACK

INTERLOGUE

ACT TWO
Scene 5: THEY FELL
Scene 6: WHERE IT WENT
Scene 7: STORY OF HOPE
Scene 8: SEEING THE THING

EPILOGUE

CHARACTERS

ALMOST, MAINE can be played by as few as four and as many as nineteen actors.

PROLOGUE
PETE and GINETTE, who have been dating for a little while.

HER HEART
EAST, a repairman, and GLORY, a hiker.

SAD AND GLAD
JIMMY, a heating and cooling guy; SANDRINE, his ex-girlfriend; a salty WAITRESS.

THIS HURTS
MARVALYN, a woman who is very good at protecting herself, and STEVE, an open, kind fellow whose brother protects him.

GETTING IT BACK
GAYLE and LENDALL, longtime girlfriend and boyfriend.

INTERLOGUE
PETE, from the "Prologue."

THEY FELL
RANDY and CHAD, two "County boys."

WHERE IT WENT
PHIL, a working man, and his hardworking wife, MARCI.

STORY OF HOPE
HOPE, who has traveled the world, and a MAN, who has not.

SEEING THE THING
RHONDA, a tough woman, and DAVE, the not-so-tough man who loves her.

EPILOGUE
PETE and GINETTE, from the "Prologue."

PLACE

Various locales in Almost, Maine, a small town in northern Maine that doesn't quite exist.

TIME

The present. Everything takes place at nine o'clock on a cold, clear, moonless, slightly surreal Friday night in the middle of the deepest part of a northern Maine winter.

ALMOST, MAINE

PROLOGUE

*Music. (Julian Fleisher's original score is highly recommended.)
It is a cold Friday night in the middle of winter in a small,
mythical town in northern Maine called Almost, Maine. A
field of stars — a clear, cold, moonless northern night sky —
serves as the backdrop for the entire play. Lights up on Pete and
Ginette sitting on a bench in Pete's yard, looking at the stars.
They are not sitting close to each other at all. Pete is sitting on
the stage right end of the bench; Ginette, on the stage left end of
the bench. Music fades. Long beat of Pete and Ginette looking
at the stars. Ginette keeps stealing glances at Pete.*

GINETTE. Pete, I — ... *(Beat. She's about to say, "I love you.")*
PETE. What?
GINETTE. *(She can't quite do it.)* I just — am having a nice time,
Pete.
PETE. I'm glad, Ginette.
GINETTE. I always do with you.
PETE. I'm glad. *(Pete and Ginette enjoy this moment together.
There's nothing else to say, so ... back to the sky.)*
GINETTE. *(Still can't say what she really wants to say.)* And the
stars are just — ! I didn't know you knew all that stuff! // After all
this time, I didn't know you knew all that!
PETE. Well, it's not — ... It's just stuff my dad taught me ...
*(Beat. There's nothing else to say, so ... back to the stars. Beat. Ginette
turns to Pete.)*
GINETTE. Pete — ...
PETE. *(Turning to Ginette.)* Yeah?
GINETTE. I love you. *(Beat. Pete just stares at Ginette. Beat. Pete
looks away from Ginette. Beat. And does not respond. Beat. Ginette*

takes in Pete's reaction; deflates; then looks away from him, trying to figure out what has happened. We now have two very uncomfortable people. Pete is dealing with what Ginette has just said to him; Ginette is dealing with Pete's response — or lack thereof — to what she has just said. Big ... long ... pause. Finally, there's nothing else for Pete to say but the truth, which is:)

PETE. I ... love you, too.

GINETTE. Oh!!! *(Huge relief! Pete and Ginette feel JOY! Ginette shivers — a happy kind of shiver.)*

PETE. Oh, are you cold? // Wanna go inside?

GINETTE. No, no. No. I just wanna sit. Like this. Close. *(Pete and Ginette shouldn't be close to each other at all — but for them, it's close.)* I feel so close to you tonight. It's nice to be close to you, Pete. *(She gets closer to him. Beat.)* It's safe. *(She gets closer to him again. Beat.)* I like being close. Like this. I mean, I can think of other ... *ways* ... of being close to you *(I.e., sex, and they enjoy this sweetly, truly — Pete probably can't believe she brought this up, but he's probably very happy that she did!)* but that's not — ... I like this right now. This kind of close. Right next to you. *(She gets even closer to him; leans right up against him. Beat.)* You know, right now, I think I'm about as close to you as I can possibly be. *(She is very content.)*

PETE. *(Beat. Honestly discovering.)* Well ... not really.

GINETTE. What?

PETE. *(He is simply and truly figuring this out.)* Not really. I mean, if you think about it in a different way, you're not really *close* to me at all. You're really actually about as far away from me as you can possibly be. I mean, if you think about it, technically — if you're assuming the world is round, like a ball, *(Gathering snow to make a snowball for use as a visual. This works pretty well when little drifts of snow are attached to the bench, with the snowball resting among the drifts.)* like a snowball, the farthest away you can be from somebody is if you're sitting right next to them. See, if I'm here *(Points out a place on the snowball that represents him.)*, and you're here *(Points out a place on the snowball that represents her, and it's right next to him — practically the same place he just pointed to.)*, then ... *(Pete now demonstrates that if you go around the world the OTHER way — all the way around the world the OTHER way, equatorially [not pole to pole] — that he and Ginette are actually as far away from each other as they can possibly be. Little beat.)* ... that's far.

GINETTE. *(Takes this in. What on earth does he mean?)* Yeah. *(Beat. Disheartened, Ginette moves away from Pete — all the way to*

the other end of the bench. She doesn't feel like being "close" anymore.)
PETE. *(Takes this in: His "interesting thought" seems to have moved the evening's proceedings in a direction he didn't intend. Then, trying to save the evening, hopeful:)* But … now you're closer. *(Because she actually is closer, the way he just described it.)*
GINETTE. *(Puzzled.)* Yeah. *(Perhaps hurt, she gets up and starts to leave. What else is there to do? After she takes barely a step or two, Pete stops her with:)*
PETE. And closer … *(Ginette stops. She turns and looks at Pete, then turns back and starts to leave, but, as she takes another step away from him, Pete again interrupts her step with:)* And closer … *(Ginette stops again. She turns and looks at Pete, then turns back and starts to leave again, but, as she does so, Pete stops her with:)* And closer … *(Ginette stops again; looks at Pete again; turns … and takes another step … and another and another and another and another. With each step she takes, Pete says, " … and closer and closer and closer and closer … " When she is just about to exit, Ginette stops. She is trying to figure out what's going on, what Pete is saying. She looks at Pete; she looks off left; looks at Pete again; looks off left again; and then leaves, taking step after step. With every single step she takes, Pete calls to her, telling her, with great hope, that she's " … closer and closer and closer and closer … " until, eventually, Ginette is gone, exiting stage left, with Pete still calling, " … and closer," with every single step she takes. Unfortunately, with every step she takes, Ginette is getting farther and farther away from Pete. This is not necessarily what Pete intended, and his "closer's" trail off. Music. Lights fade on a sad, confused, helpless Pete. He looks at his snowball. What has he done? And we begin …*

ACT ONE

with Scene One, which is entitled ...

HER HEART

Music fades. The lights fade up on a woman standing in the front yard of an old farmhouse in Almost, Maine. She is clutching a small brown paper grocery bag to her chest. She is looking up at the sky. A porch light comes on. We hear a screen door open and slam as a man enters. He watches the woman for a while. He is wearing a big warm coat over plaid pajamas, and slippers or untied boots.

MAN. Hello.

WOMAN. *(To him.)* Hello. *(Resumes looking to the sky.)*

MAN. I thought I saw someone. *(Little beat.)* I was about to go to bed. I saw you from my window ... *(Beat.)* Can I — ? ... Is there something I can do for you?

WOMAN. *(To him.)* Oh, no. I'm just here to see the northern lights. *(Back to the sky.)*

MAN. Okay. Okay. It's just — it's awful late and you're in my yard ...

WOMAN. Oh, I hope you don't mind! I'll only be here tonight. I'll see them tonight. The northern lights. And then I'll be gone. I hope you don't mind —

MAN. *(Looking out.)* Is that your tent? *(The tent should be seen by East and Glory — not by the audience.)*

WOMAN. Yes.

MAN. You've pitched a tent ... >

WOMAN. So I have a place to sleep, >

MAN. in my yard ...

WOMAN. after I see them, I hope you don't mind.

MAN. Well, it's not that I —

WOMAN. Do you mind?

MAN. Well, I don't know if —

WOMAN. Oh, no, I think you mind!

MAN. No, it's not that I mind —

WOMAN. No, you do! You *do!* Oh, I'm so sorry! I didn't think you would! I didn't think — . You see, it says in your brochure >

MAN. My brochure?

WOMAN. that people from Maine wouldn't mind. It says *(Pulling out a brochure about Maine tourism.)* that people from Maine are different, that they live life "the way life *should* be,"[*] and that, "in the tradition of their brethren in rural northern climes, like Scandinavia," that they'll let people who are complete strangers, like cross-country skiers and bikers and hikers, camp out in their yard, if they need to, for nothing, they'll just let you. I'm a hiker. Is it true? >

MAN. Well —

WOMAN. that they'll just let you stay in their yards if you need to? 'Cause I need to. Camp out. 'Cause I'm where I need to be. This is the farthest I've ever traveled — I'm from a part of the country that's a little closer to things — never been this far north before, or east, and did you know that Maine is the only state in the country that's attached to only one other state?!?

MAN. Um —

WOMAN. It is!! *(Taking in all the open space.)* Feels like the end of the world, and here I am at the end of the world, and I have nowhere to go, so I was counting on staying here, unless it's not true, I mean, *is* it true? >

MAN. Well —

WOMAN. Would you let a hiker who was where she needed to be just camp out in your yard for free? >

MAN. Well —

WOMAN. I mean, if a person really needed to, >

MAN. Well —

WOMAN. reallyreally needed to?

MAN. Well, if a person really needed to, sure, but —

WOMAN. *(Huge relief!)* Oh, I'm so glad, then!! Thank you!! *(The woman goes to the man, throws her arms open, and hugs him. In the hug, the bag gets squished between their bodies. When they part, the man is holding the woman's bag. The exchange of the bag is almost imperceptible to both the man and the woman, and to the audience.*

---

[*] If you ever go to Maine by car, via Interstate 95, you will be greeted by a sign, erected by the Maine Office of Tourism, that reads: "Maine: The Way Life Should Be."

Immediately after hugging the man, the woman resumes looking intently for the northern lights. Beat. Then, realizing she doesn't have her bag:) Oh, my gosh! *(Realizing that the man has her bag.)* I need that!

MAN. Oh. Here. *(He gives it back.)*

WOMAN. Thank you. *(The woman resumes looking to the sky.)*

MAN. Sure. *(Beat.)* Okay — . Okay ... *(Beat.)* So you're just lookin' for a place to see the northern lights from?

WOMAN. Yeah. Just tonight.

MAN. Well, you know, you might not see 'em tonight, 'cause // you never really know if —

WOMAN. Oh, no. I'll see them. Because I'm in a good place: Your latitude is *good*. And this is the right time: Solar activity is at an eleven-year peak. Everything's in order. And, boy, you have good sky for it. *(Taking in the sky.)* There's lots of sky here.

MAN. Used to be a potato farm.

WOMAN. I was gonna say — no trees in the way. And it's *flat!* Makes for a big sky! *(Beat.)* So — you're a farmer?

MAN. No. Used to be a farm. I'm a repairman.

WOMAN. Oh.

MAN. Fix things.

WOMAN. Oh. *(Laughs.)*

MAN. What?

WOMAN. You're not a lobster man.

MAN. No ...

WOMAN. I guess I thought that everyone from Maine was a lobster man and talked in that funny ... way like they do in Maine, and you don't talk that way ...

MAN. Nope. You're not Down East. You're up north. And this is how we talk up north, pretty much.

WOMAN. Oh.

MAN. Plus, ocean's a couple hundred miles away. Be an awful long ride to work if I was a lobsterman.

WOMAN. *(Enjoying him.)* Yeah. Well, anyway, thank you. Thank you for letting me stay. I've had a bad enough time of things lately not to be given a bad time here — *(The man, inexplicably drawn to her, kisses the woman. When they break, the bag has exchanged clutches imperceptibly — the man has it. And now we have two stunned people.)*

MAN. Oh ...

WOMAN. *(Trying to figure out what just happened.)* Um ...

MAN. Oh.

WOMAN. Um ...

MAN. Oh, boy.

WOMAN. Um …

MAN. I'm sorry. I just — … I think I love you.

WOMAN. Really.

MAN. *(Perplexed.)* Yeah. I saw you from my window and … I love you.

WOMAN. Well … — that's very nice — … but there's something I think you should know: I'm not here for that.

MAN. Oh, no! I didn't think you were!

WOMAN. I'm here to pay my respects. To my *husband.*

MAN. Oh —

WOMAN. Yeah: My *husband.* Wes. I just wanted to say goodbye to him, 'cause he died recently. On Tuesday, actually. And, see, the northern lights — did you know this? — the northern lights are really the torches that the recently departed carry with them so they can find their way to heaven, and, see, it takes three days for a soul to make its way home, to heaven, and this is Friday! This is the third day, so, you see, I *will* see them, the northern lights, because they're *him:* He'll be carrying one of the torches. And, see, I didn't leave things well with him, so I was just hoping I could come here and say goodbye to him and not be bothered, but what you did there just a second ago, that bothered me, I think, and I'm not here for that, so maybe I should go // and find another yard —

MAN. No! No! I'm sorry if I — … if I've behaved in a way that I shouldn't have —

WOMAN. *(Leaving.)* No //, I think —

MAN. No! I really don't know what happened.

WOMAN. Well, *I* do, I know what happened!

MAN. I'm not the kind of person who does things like that. Please. Don't go. Just — do what you need to do. I won't bother you. Maybe just … consider what I did a very warm Maine welcome.

WOMAN. *(Stopping; charmed.)* All right. All right. *(Beat.)* I'm — . My name's Glory.

MAN. I'm East. For Easton. It's the name of the town — little ways that way — where I was born. Mess-up on the birth certificate … "a son, Easton, born on this sixth day of January, *[insert appropriate year]* in the town of Matthew, Maine" … instead of the other way around …

GLORY. *(Amused.)* Aw, I'm sorry … >

EAST. Naw …

GLORY. so, *(Referring to the place.)* Easton, >

19

EAST. Yeah —

GLORY. yeah! I passed through near there on my way here, and, by the way, *(Scanning the horizon.)* where is "here," where am I? I couldn't find it on my map.

EAST. Um … Almost.

GLORY. What?

EAST. You're in unorganized territory. Township Thirteen, Range Seven. *(Glory checks her map.)* It's not gonna be on your map, cause it's not an actual town, technically.

GLORY. What // do you mean —

EAST. See, to be a town, you gotta get organized. And we never got around to gettin' organized, so … we're just Almost.

GLORY. Oh … *(They enjoy this. Beat. Glory now deals with the fact that she is missing her bag. She was clutching it to her chest, and now it's gone. This should upset her so much that it seems like it affects her breathing.)* Oh! Oh!

EAST. What? What's wrong?

GLORY. *(Seeming to be having trouble breathing.)* My heart!

EAST. What? Are you // okay?

GLORY. My heart! *(Seeing that he has her bag; pointing to the bag.)*

EAST. What?

GLORY. You have my *heart!*

EAST. I — ?

GLORY. In that bag, it's in that bag! >

EAST. Oh.

GLORY. Please give it back, // please! It's my heart. I need it. Please!

EAST. Okay, okay, okay. *(He gives her the bag.)*

GLORY. Thank you. *(Her breathing normalizes.)*

EAST. You're welcome. *(A long beat while East considers what he has just heard.)* I'm sorry, did you just say that … your heart is in that bag?, is that what you just said?, that // your heart — …?

GLORY. Yes.

EAST. *(Considers.)* It's heavy.

GLORY. Yes.

EAST. *(Beat.)* Why is it in that bag?

GLORY. It's how I carry it around.

EAST. Why?

GLORY. It's broken.

EAST. What happened?

GLORY. Wes broke it.

20

EAST. Your husband?

GLORY. Yeah. He went away.

EAST. Oh.

GLORY. With someone else.

EAST. Oh, I'm sorry.

GLORY. Yeah. And when he did that, I felt like my heart would break. And that's exactly what happened. It broke: hardened up and cracked in two. Hurt so bad, I had to go to the hospital, and when I got there, they told me they were gonna have to take it out. And when they took it out, they dropped it on the floor and it broke into nineteen pieces. Slate. *(Gently shakes the bag, which should be filled with small [a heart is the size of its owner's fist] pieces of slate — they make a great sound when shaken.)* It turned to slate. *(Beat. She looks back up at the sky.)*

EAST. *(Takes this in. Beat. His only response to what she has just told him is:)* Great for roofing. *(Glory just looks at East. Beat. Then:)* Wait a second, how do you breathe? If your heart is in that bag, how are you alive?

GLORY. *(Indicating the heart that's now in her chest.)* Artificial …

EAST. Really.

GLORY. Yeah. 'Cause my real one's broken.

EAST. Then — why do you carry it around with you?

GLORY. It's my *heart.*

EAST. But it's broken.

GLORY. Yeah.

EAST. 'Cause your husband left you.

GLORY. Yeah.

EAST. Well, why are you paying your respects to him if he left you?

GLORY. Because that's what you do when a person dies, you pay them respects —

EAST. But he left you, >

GLORY. Yeah, but —

EAST. and it seems to me that a man who leaves somebody doesn't deserve any respects.

GLORY. *(Deflecting.)* Well, I just didn't leave things well with him, >

EAST. *(Pressing.)* What do you mean? —

GLORY. and I need to apologize to him.

EAST. But he *left* you! >

GLORY. I know, but I —

21

EAST. Why should you apologize?

GLORY. Because!

EAST. Because why?!?

GLORY. Because I killed him!

EAST. Oh. *(This stops East; he backs off a bit.)*

GLORY. And I'd like to apologize. *(Beat. Then, admission:)* See, he had come to visit me when I was in recovery from when they put my artificial heart in — I was almost better; I was just about to go home, too — and he said he wanted me back. And I said, "Wes, I have a new heart now. I'm sorry … It doesn't want you back … " And that just killed him.

EAST. *(Relief.)* Oh. But, it didn't kill him, you didn't *kill* him —

GLORY. Yes, I did! Because he got so sad that my new heart didn't want him back, that he just tore outta the hospital, and … an ambulance that was comin' in from an emergency didn't see him and just … took him right out, and if I'd have been able to take him back, >

EAST. Glory —

GLORY. he wouldn't have torn outta there like that, >

EAST. Glory!

GLORY. and been just taken out like that, and so, I just feel that, for closure, the right thing to do is — *(Inexplicably drawn to her, East kisses Glory. When she pulls away, he has her heart again. She takes it back.)* Please don't do that anymore.

EAST. Why?, I love you!

GLORY. Well, don't.

EAST. Why?

GLORY. Because I won't be able to love you back: I have a heart that can pump my blood and that's all. The one that does the other stuff is broken. It doesn't work anymore. *(Again, inexplicably drawn to her, East deliberately kisses Glory. Glory pulls away. East has her heart again. Glory grabs it from him; East grabs it right back.)*

EAST. Please let me have this.

GLORY. *(Desperately trying to get her heart back.)* No! It's mine!

EAST. *(Keeping her heart.)* I can fix it!

GLORY. I don't know if I want you to!

EAST. Glory — !

GLORY. *(Going after her heart.)* East, please give that back to me!

EAST. *(Keeping her heart.)* But, it's broken. >

GLORY. Please — !

EAST. It's no good like this.

GLORY. But, it's my heart, East!

EAST. Yes, it is. And I believe *I* have it. *(This stops Glory. Beat.)* And I can fix it. *(Beat.)* I'm a repairman. I repair things. It's what I do. *(Beat. East crouches, gently places the bag on the ground, and starts to open it in order to examine its contents. Music. As he opens the bag, music up, and the northern lights appear — in front of Glory, above Glory, on the field of stars behind Glory. Glory sees them ... and they're a thing of wonder.)*
GLORY. Oh! Oh, wow! Oh, wow! Oh, they're so beautiful ... *(Remembering who they are.)* Oh! Oh! — Wes!! Wes!! Goodbye! I'm so sorry! ... Goodbye, Wes! *(And the northern lights — and Wes — are gone. Glory turns to East, who has taken a little piece of her heart out of the bag, and is examining it. Music out. Then, in the clear:)* Hello, East. *(Music continues. East looks at Glory, and then begins repairing her heart ... as the lights fade. Transitional aurora. End of "Her Heart." After the lights have faded and "Her Heart" is over, we begin Scene Two, which is entitled ...*

SAD AND GLAD

Music fades. Lights fade up on Jimmy sitting alone at a table in a back corner of Almost, Maine's local hang-out, the Moose Paddy. He is nursing a couple of Buds. Sandrine enters. She is coming from the ladies' room and is cheerily heading back to her friends, who are up front. She passes Jimmy. Jimmy sees Sandrine, stops her.

JIMMY. Sandrine!
SANDRINE. Hmm? *(Beat. This is a bit awkward — awful, actually. Then, overcompensating:)* Jimmy!
JIMMY. Hey!
SANDRINE. Hey!
JIMMY. Hey!!
SANDRINE. Hey!!
JIMMY/SANDRINE. *(Jimmy hugs Sandrine. Sandrine doesn't really take the hug or hug him back.)* Heyyyy!!!
JIMMY. How you doin'?!?
SANDRINE. Doin' pretty good! How are you doin'?!?

23

JIMMY. I'm good, I'm good! How are ya?!?

SANDRINE. I'm good, doin' good, great! How are you?

JIMMY. Great, great! How are ya?

SANDRINE. Great, // great!

JIMMY. Oh, that's great!

SANDRINE. Yeah!

JIMMY. That's great!

SANDRINE. Yeah!

JIMMY. That's great!

SANDRINE. Yeah.

JIMMY. That's great!

SANDRINE. Yeah.

JIMMY. That's great!

SANDRINE. Yeah.

JIMMY. You look great!

SANDRINE. Oh …

JIMMY. You look great.

SANDRINE. Thanks.

JIMMY. You do. You look so great.

SANDRINE. Thanks, Jimmy.

JIMMY. So pretty. So pretty.

SANDRINE. Thanks. *(Beat.)*

JIMMY. Here, have a seat.

SANDRINE. Oh, Jimmy, I can't —

JIMMY. Aw, come on, I haven't seen you in … well, *months* …

SANDRINE. Yeah.

JIMMY. … and months and months and months and months and months and months and *months*, how does that happen? Live in the same town as someone and never see 'em? >

SANDRINE. I don't know …

JIMMY. I mean, I haven't seen you since that night before that morning when I woke up and you were just gone.

SANDRINE. Yeah, I —

WAITRESS. *(Entering.)* Look at you two, tucked away in the corner over here. Lucky I found ya! *(Referring to Jimmy's couple of Buds.)* Is the man and his lovely lady ready for another round?

JIMMY/SANDRINE. Well — / No! We're not together.

JIMMY/SANDRINE. We'll — / We're all set, thanks.

JIMMY/SANDRINE. Yeah — / All set!

JIMMY. Yeah.

WAITRESS. Okay. Well, holler if you need anything.

SANDRINE. Thanks.

WAITRESS. No really — you gotta holler. It's busy up front! *(She exits.)*

SANDRINE. Okay.

JIMMY. *(Fishing.)* So … You here with anybody, or —

SANDRINE. Yeah, the girls.

JIMMY. Oh.

SANDRINE. We're, uh — … *(Covering.)* Girls' night! We're in the front. Actually, I just had to use the ladies' room, so I should get back to // them.

JIMMMY: Aw, but I haven't seen ya! They'll survive without ya for a minute or two! So, what's been — here *(Offering her a seat.)* — what's been goin' on, whatcha been up to? >

SANDRINE. *(Giving in, sitting.)* Well —

JIMMY. Did you know that I took over Dad's business?

SANDRINE. Yeah, that's great …

JIMMY. I run it now, >

SANDRINE. I heard that.

JIMMY. I'm runnin' it, >

SANDRINE. Heard that.

JIMMY. runnin' the business, >

SANDRINE. Congratula>

JIMMY. runnin' the whole show, >

SANDRINE. tions, good for you, good for you.

JIMMY. the whole shebang, thanks, yeah. We still do heating and cooling, >

SANDRINE. Yeah?

JIMMY. and we've expanded, too, we do rugs now, we shampoo 'em.

SANDRINE. Oh.

JIMMY. It's a lotta work. A lotta work. I'm on call a lot: weekends, holidays, you name it, 'cause, you know, your heat goes, people die, it's serious.

SANDRINE. Yeah.

JIMMY. Yeah. Like, I do Thanksgivin', Christmas, 'cause I let the guys who work for me, like, East helps with repairs sometimes, I let 'em have the day off so they can be with their families since I'm all alone this year.

SANDRINE. Oh.

JIMMY. Yeah. *(Driving the point home.)* I really don't have any-body anymore, really. My brother and sister got canned, so they left town, and >

SANDRINE. Right —

JIMMY. Mom and Dad retired, headed south.

SANDRINE. Yeah, I heard that.

JIMMY. Vermont.

SANDRINE. Oh.

JIMMY. Yeah, winters there are a lot easier. And then Spot went and died on me …

SANDRINE. Oh, Jimmy, I didn't know that …

JIMMY. Yeah. He was old, it was his time, he was a good fish though, but, so, like I said, I really don't have anybody anymore, really … but, so, um, I was wonderin' — would you like to come over? It'd be fun! Catch up, hang out?

SANDRINE. Oh —

WAITRESS. *(Entering.)* And I forgot to tell ya — don't forget: Friday night special at The Moose Paddy: Drink free if you're sad. So, if you're sad, or if you two little lovebirds are ready for another coupla Buds or somethin', you just let me know, all right?

SANDRINE. No, we're —

JIMMY. Okay.

WAITRESS. Okay. *(She exits.)*

SANDRINE. *(To waitress.)* Okay. *(Beat.)*

JIMMY. So whatta you say? Wanna come on over, for fun —

SANDRINE. No, Jimmy. I can't. I can't. *(Getting up to leave.)* I really gotta get back with the girls.

JIMMY. Naw —

SANDRINE. *(Forceful, but kind.)* Yeah, Jimmy, yeah. I gotta. 'Cause, see … oh, gosh, I've been meanin' to tell you this for a while: There's a guy, Jimmy. I've got a guy.

JIMMY. *(Huge blow. But he's tough.)* Oh.

SANDRINE. Yeah.

JIMMY. Well … good for you. Gettin' yourself out there again.

SANDRINE. Yeah.

JIMMY. Movin' on …

SANDRINE. Yeah, well, actually, Jimmy, it's more than me just gettin' myself out there and movin' on. Um … this is my … bachelorette party. *(Beat. Then, off his blank look:)* I'm gettin' married.

JIMMY. *(Huger blow.)* Oh.

SANDRINE. Yeah.

JIMMY. Wow.

SANDRINE. Yeah.

JIMMY. Wow.

SANDRINE. Yeah.

JIMMY. Wow.

SANDRINE. Yeah.

JIMMY. Wow. That's — ... Thought you said you weren't gonna do that. Get married. Thought it wasn't for you, you told me. *(Beat.)* Guess it just wasn't for you with me. *(Beat.)* So, who's ... who's the lucky guy?

SANDRINE. Martin Laferriere. *(Say, "la-FAIRY-AIR.")* You know him? The uh —

JIMMY. The ranger guy, over in Ashland.

SANDRINE. Yeah, yeah, yeah!

JIMMY. Wow.

SANDRINE. Yeah.

JIMMY. He's a legend. Legendary. I mean, if you're lost on a mountain in Maine, he's the guy you want lookin' for you.

SANDRINE. Yeah.

JIMMY. I mean, if you're lost out there in this big bad northern world, Martin La*ferriere's* the guy you want to have go out there and find you.

SANDRINE. Yeah.

JIMMY. And he ... found you.

SANDRINE. Yeah. I'm sorry I never told you — I actually thought you woulda known, I thought you would have heard ...

JIMMY. How would I have heard?

SANDRINE. Well, you know ... people talk.

JIMMY. Not about things they know you don't wanna hear, they don't. And I gotta be honest ... that's not somethin' I woulda wanted to hear... *(Beat.)* So ... when's the big event?

SANDRINE. Um ... tomorrow!

JIMMY. Really.

SANDRINE. Yup!

JIMMY. Well then ... *(Jimmy downs his Bud, and then raises his arm, to get the waitress' attention. As he does so, his unbuttoned sleeve slides up his arm a little. He hollers:)* HEY!

SANDRINE. *(Not wanting Jimmy to draw attention to them.)* What are you doin'?

JIMMY. *(Going towards the front.)* Gettin' our waitress, she said holler, *(Calling to waitress.)* HEY! *(To Sandrine.)* What's her name?

SANDRINE. I don't know, she's new // here.

JIMMY. *(To waitress.)* HEY!

SANDRINE. What are you doin'?

JIMMY. We gotta celebrate! You got found! And you deserve it!

He's quite a guy.

SANDRINE. Aw, Jimmy.

JIMMY. And so are you.

SANDRINE. *(That was the nicest thing a guy like Jimmy could say to a girl.)* Jimmy ...

JIMMY. *(Arm raised, hollering to waitress.)* HEY!

SANDRINE. *(Protesting.)* Jimmy! *(Then, noticing a black marking on Jimmy's arm.)* Jimmy!-whoa-hey! What's that?

JIMMY. *(To Sandrine.)* What?

SANDRINE. That. *(Referring to the black marking on his arm.)*

JIMMY. *(Covering the mark, using his other arm to wave down the waitress; to Sandrine.)* Oh, nothin', tattoo, *(To waitress.)* HEY!

SANDRINE. What?!?

JIMMY. *(To Sandrine.)* Tattoo. *(To waitress.)* HEY!

SANDRINE. *(Intrigued.)* What — When did you get that?

JIMMY. *(To Sandrine.)* Um ... After you left, *(To waitress.)* HEY!

SANDRINE. *(Intrigued, going for his arm.)* Jimmy! Well — what's it of, what's it say?

JIMMY. *(To Sandrine.)* Nothin', nothin', *(To waitress.)* hey-hey-HEY! *(Sandrine grabs his arm.)* N-no!

SANDRINE. *(She rolls up his sleeve and takes a beat as she reads, on the inside of his forearm, in big, bold letters:)* "Villian." *(Rhymes with "Jillian.")*

JIMMY. *Villain.*

SANDRINE. Who's Villian?

JIMMY. *Villain.* It's supposed to say, "Villain."

SANDRINE. What?

JIMMY. It's supposed to say, "Villain."

SANDRINE. Well, it doesn't say, "Villain." It says, "Villian."

JIMMY. I know, I spelled it wrong — >

SANDRINE. What?!?

JIMMY. They spelled it wrong. It says, "Villian," but it's supposed to say, "Villain."

SANDRINE. Well, why is it supposed to say, "Villain"? Why would you want a tattoo that says, "Villain"?

JIMMY. 'Cause ...

SANDRINE. 'Cause why?

JIMMY. Just 'cause.

SANDRINE. Just 'cause *why?*

JIMMY. Just 'cause ... when a guy's got a girl like you ... Well, I just think that losin' a girl like you, drivin' a girl like you away ... >

SANDRINE. Jimmy, you didn't drive me away —

JIMMY. is just plain criminal. It's criminal. It's *villainy*! And it should be punished! So I punished myself. I marked myself a villain. So girls would stay away. So I'd never have to go through … what I went through with you. Again. Can I kiss you?

SANDRINE. *(Not mean.)* No. *(Beat. She kisses Jimmy on the cheek. Beat. Then, referring to his tattoo:)* You can get that undone, you know.

JIMMY. Yeah. *(Beat.)*

SANDRINE. I gotta head. *(She goes.)*

JIMMY. Yeah. *(Then, stopping Sandrine.)* I'm — . *(Sandrine stops, turns to Jimmy. Beat.)* I'm glad you got found.

SANDRINE. Thanks, Jimmy. *(Sandrine goes back to her bachelorette party — and she is welcomed back heartily. We hear this. Jimmy hears this. He is alone, sad, and stuck there. Maybe he gets his coat off his chair. Time to go home. Alone. As usual. Beat.)*

WAITRESS. *(Entering.)* Hey! Sorry! You were wavin' me down. I saw you, but it's so busy in the front! There's this bachelorette party: those *girls!* Good thing it's not, "Drink free if you're *glad*," 'cause those girls are wicked *glad*. Gosh — had to fight my way through to find you, but I did it! I found ya! So: What'd ya need, what can I do ya for? Another Bud?

JIMMY. Um … *(He's sad, looking off to where Sandrine went.)*

WAITRESS. *(Looks off to where Sandrine went … sees the empty chair … puts the pieces together.)* Oh, pal … Um … Um … Well, remember, like I said, Moose Paddy special: Drinks are free if you're sad. Okay? Just tell me you're sad, and you'll drink free. *(Beat.)* Just say the word. Let me know. 'Cause I know from sad, and you're lookin' pretty sad. *(No response from Jimmy. He's just sad.)* Okay. Well, my name's Villian, if you need anything. *(Note to actress playing Villian: The next line may be used if you feel you need it for clarity. It's just a backup, in case you feel the first mention of your name isn't heard, or if the audience is slow to catch on. Use it if you need it; don't if you don't — up to you!)* Just ask for Villian. *(She goes.)*

JIMMY. *(Beat. Her name registers. He calls to her.)* Villian!?!

VILLIAN. *(She stops.)* Yeah?

JIMMY. Hi.

VILLIAN. Hi …

JIMMY. I'm not sad. I just would like another Bud.

VILLIAN. All right! *(She goes.)*

JIMMY. Villian!!
VILLIAN. *(Stopping.)* Yeah?!?
JIMMY. I'm glad you found me.
VILLIAN. Aw … *(Leaving, to herself:)* "I'm glad you found me," that's adorable … *(Music. Looks like Jimmy might stay. Maybe he's a little glad. He sits back down, maybe deals with his tattooed forearm in some way. Lights fade. Transitional aurora. End of "Sad and Glad." After the lights have faded and "Sad and Glad" is over, we begin Scene Three, which is entitled …*

THIS HURTS

Music fades. Lights come up on a woman finishing up iron-ing a man's clothes, in the laundry room of Ma Dudley's Boarding House in Almost, Maine. A man is sitting on a bench. The woman starts folding the man's shirt she was iron-ing, but thinks better of it, and instead, deliberately crumples it, and throws it into her laundry basket. She picks up the iron, wraps the cord around it, preparing to put it away. As she does so, she burns herself on it.

WOMAN. Ow! Dammit! *(The man takes note of this and writes "iron" in a homemade book labeled "Things That Can Hurt You." Meanwhile, the woman has exited to return the iron to its proper place. She returns to deal with the ironing board, which also must be returned to its proper place — the same place she just brought the iron. After folding up the ironing board, she turns to exit and accidentally wallops the man in the head with the ironing board, knocking him off the bench he was sitting on.)* Oh, no! I'm sorry! I'm sorry! Oh … I didn't see you, are you okay?!?
MAN. *(Unfazed.)* Yeah.
WOMAN. No you're not!! I smashed you with the ironing board, I wasn't even looking! Are you hurt?
MAN. No.
WOMAN. Oh, you must be!! I just *smashed* you! Where did I get you?
MAN. In the head.

WOMAN. In the head!?! Oh, *(Going to him.)* come here, are you okay?

MAN. Is there any blood?

WOMAN. No.

MAN. Any discoloration?

WOMAN. No.

MAN. Then I'm okay.

WOMAN. Well, I'm gonna go get you some ice.

MAN. No. I can't feel things like that.

WOMAN. Like what?

MAN. Like when I get smashed in the head with an ironing board. I don't get hurt.

WOMAN. What?

MAN. I can't feel pain.

WOMAN. Oh, Jeezum Crow *(Say, "JEE-zum CROW" — it's a euphemism.),* what the hell have I done to you? >

MAN. Nothin' —

WOMAN. You're talkin' loopy, listen to you, goin' on about not being able to feel pain, that's delusional, I've knocked the sense right outta ya!

MAN. No, I'm okay.

WOMAN. Shh! Listen: I was gonna be a nurse, so I know: You're hurt. You just took a good shot right to the head, and that's serious.

MAN. No, it's not serious. I don't think an ironing board could really hurt your head, 'cause, see, *(Forcing his "Things That Can Hurt You" book on her.)* ironing boards aren't on my list of things that can hurt you, >

WOMAN. *(Dealing with his book.)* What is — ?

MAN. plus, there's no blood or discoloration from where I got hit, so ... >

WOMAN. Well, you can be hurt and not be bleeding or bruised —

MAN. And my list is pretty reliable, 'cause my brother Paul is helping me make it, and I can prove it to you: See, I bet if I took this ironing board, like this, and hit you with it, that it wouldn't hurt you *(He smashes her in the head with the ironing board.),* see?, // that didn't hurt.

WOMAN. OW!! *(Scrambling to get away from him.)*

MAN. Oh!

WOMAN. Ow! What the hell was that?! // Why did you do that?

MAN. Oh! I'm sorry. // Did that hurt?

WOMAN. God!

MAN. Oh, it did, didn't it?

WOMAN. Ow!

MAN. Oh, I didn't think it would 'cause, see, ironing boards are not on my list of things that can hurt you, but, gosh, maybe they should be on my list, because —

WOMAN. What are you talkin' about?

MAN. I have a list of things that can hurt you, my brother Paul is helping me make it, and ironing boards aren't on it.

WOMAN. Well, that ironing board hurt me.

MAN. Yeah.

WOMAN. So you should add it to your list.

MAN. Yeah. *(Beat. He adds "ironing boards" to his list of "Things That Can Hurt You." He then picks up a book labeled "Things to Be Afraid Of.")* Should I be *afraid* of ironing boards?

WOMAN. Well, if someone swings it at your head and wallops you with it, yes …

MAN. Well, it's not — I have a list of things to be afraid of, too — and ironing boards are not on this list either.

WOMAN. Well they shouldn't be, really.

MAN. No?

WOMAN. No, you shouldn't be *afraid* of ironing boards.

MAN. No?

WOMAN. No.

MAN. But they can *hurt* you.

WOMAN. Yeah.

MAN. So I should be *afraid* of them.

WOMAN. No.

MAN. So I *shouldn't* be afraid of them?

WOMAN. Right.

MAN. But they can *hurt* me.

WOMAN. Well, if they're used the way you used it, yeah.

MAN. Oh-oh-oh! So, they're kind of like the opposite of God!

WOMAN. What?

MAN. Well, ironing boards can *hurt* me, but I shouldn't be *afraid* of them, but God, my brother Paul says, God *won't* hurt me, but I should *fear* him.

WOMAN. I guess.

MAN. Boy, this is getting very complicated.

WOMAN. What is?

MAN. This business of learning what hurts, what doesn't hurt, what to be afraid of, what not to be afraid of.

WOMAN. Are you sure you're okay?, // you're just goin' on and on about crazy stuff —

MAN. Oh, yeah, yeah, see, I have congenital analgesia, he thinks. Some // people —

WOMAN. What?

MAN. Congenital analgesia.

WOMAN. Who thinks?

MAN. My brother Paul. Some people call it hereditary sensory neuropathy type four, but … it just means I can't feel pain. You can hit me if you want to, to see!

WOMAN. No.

MAN. Go ahead. It won't hurt. See? *(He hits his head with the book. Composition books work pretty well, because they make a great sound and don't actually hurt!)*

WOMAN. OW!

MAN. See? *(He hits his head again.)*

WOMAN. OW!

MAN. See? *(Hits his head again.)*

WOMAN. OW!

MAN. Go ahead. *(He offers her the book labeled "Things That Can Hurt You" so she can hit him with it.)*

WOMAN. No!

MAN. Come on!

WOMAN. No!!

MAN. Come on!

WOMAN. NO!!

MAN. Okay. You don't have to. Most people don't. Hit me. Most people just go away. You can go away, too, if you want to. That's what most people do when I tell them about myself. My brother Paul says I just shouldn't tell people about myself, because I scare them, *(Referring to his book labeled "Things to Be Afraid Of" so he can show her.)* so I've actually recently put "myself" on my list of things to be afraid of, but — *(Her curiosity getting the better of her, the woman comes up from behind the man and wallops him on the back of the head with the book labeled "Things That Can Hurt You.")*

WOMAN. Oh, my gosh! I'm sorry! // Oh, my gosh! I just clocked you! >

MAN. You hit me! Most people go away, but you hit me!

WOMAN. I had to *see [what would happen]!* But — are you okay?

MAN. Yeah, I don't feel // pain!

WOMAN. … Don't feel pain, right, of course you're okay! — but

33

— are you sure?

MAN. Well, is there any blood?

WOMAN. No.

MAN. Any discoloration?

WOMAN. No.

MAN. Then I'm okay.

WOMAN. Well, buddy, you can be hurt and not even look like it.

MAN. But —

WOMAN. Trust me. There are things that hurt you that make you bruised and bloody and there are things that hurt you that don't make you bruised and bloody and … they all hurt. *(Beat. Then, giving him back the book labeled "Things That Can Hurt You":)* I'm Marvalyn.

MAN. I'm Steve. I live on the third floor. Room Eleven.

MARVALYN. *(Deflecting.)* I live with my boyfriend, Eric. I love him very much.

STEVE. Yeah. We saw you move in.

MARVALYN. Yeah. Our roof collapsed from all the snow in December. We're just here until we can get our feet back on the ground.

STEVE. Oh. Well, that's good, 'cause that's what Ma Dudley says her boarding house is. A place where people can live until they get their feet back on the ground. My brother Paul says we've been trying to get our feet back on the ground our whole lives.

MARVALYN. Oh.

STEVE. Yeah, it takes some people longer to do that than others.

MARVALYN. Yeah. *(Beat.)*

STEVE. You guys are loud.

MARVALYN. Huh?

STEVE. You and Eric. You yell and bang. We're right below you.

MARVALYN. Oh. Sorry about that. We're goin' through a rough patch. Happens. Sorry. *(Beat. Then, changing the subject:)* What is it like?

STEVE. What?

MARVALYN. To not feel pain.

STEVE. I don't know. I don't know what it's like to hurt, so … I don't know. I don't really feel.

MARVALYN. Is this … how you were born?

STEVE. Yeah. I don't have fully developed pain sensors. They're immature, my brother Paul says //, and because they're immature —

34

MARVALYN. How does he know that?

STEVE. Oh, he *reads*, >

MARVALYN. But —

STEVE. and because they're immature, my development as a human being has been retarded, he says, >

MARVALYN. But —

STEVE. but he *teaches* me what hurts, though.

MARVALYN. Why??

STEVE. So I won't ruin myself. I have to know what hurts, so I know when to be afraid. See, my mind can't tell me when to be afraid, 'cause my body doesn't know what being hurt is, so I have to memorize what might hurt.

MARVALYN. Okay …

STEVE. And I have to memorize what to be afraid of. *(Showing her, in his book.)* Things like bears. And guns and knives. And fire. And fear — I should fear fear itself — and pretty girls …

MARVALYN. Pretty girls?

STEVE. *(He thinks she's pretty.)* Yeah.

MARVALYN. Why should you be afraid of pretty girls?

STEVE. Well, 'cause my brother Paul says they can hurt you 'cause they make you love them, and that's something I'm sup-posed to be afraid of, too — love — but Paul says that I'm really lucky, 'cause I'll probably never have to deal with love, because I have a lot of deficiencies and not very many capacities as a result of the congenital analgesia.

MARVALYN. Wait, what do you mean you're never gonna have to deal with love //, why —

STEVE. 'Cause I'm never gonna know what it feels like, Paul says.

MARVALYN. Well, how does he know that?

STEVE. 'Cause it hurts.

MARVALYN. It shouldn't.

STEVE. And, plus, I have a lot of deficiencies and not very many capacities.

MARVALYN. You know what, a lot of people do. *(She kisses him. At first it's just Marvalyn kissing Steve, but, eventually, Steve partici-pates. Then Marvalyn breaks away.)* I'm sorry. I'm sorry. I'm so sorry. Are you all right? Are you okay?

STEVE. *(Doesn't quite know how to respond. He hasn't learned about this. Then, maybe feeling his lips, and resorting to his usual way of answering this question.)* Well … is there any blood?

MARVALYN. No …

STEVE. Any discoloration?

MARVALYN. No.

STEVE. Then I'm all right. *(Is he?)*

MARVALYN. Yeah. You are. *(Beat.)* I'm so sorry I did that. It's just — … You're just very sweet.

STEVE. *(Trying to make sense of what just happened.)* But … you have a boyfriend and you love him very much.

MARVALYN. *(She begins gathering her stuff.)* Yes I do. And yes I do.

STEVE. And you just kissed me.

MARVALYN. Yes I did.

STEVE. And it's Friday night and you're doing your laundry.

MARVALYN. Yes I am.

STEVE. And people who are in love with each other, they don't kiss other people and do their laundry on Friday nights, I've learned that. People who are in love with each other, they go to The Moose Paddy on Friday nights, or they go dancing together, or they go skating. And they kiss each other. They don't kiss other people — you know what? I don't think that's love, // what you and your boyfriend have —

MARVALYN. *(Deflecting, preparing to leave.)* I've been down here longer than I said I would be and he doesn't like that.

STEVE. Who?

MARVALYN. My boyfriend.

STEVE. Who you love very much.

MARVALYN. Yes.

STEVE. Even though you kissed me?

MARVALYN. Yes.

STEVE. Wow, I'm going to have to talk to my brother Paul about this —

MARVALYN. No! Don't talk to your brother Paul about this! Tell him to stop teaching you.

STEVE. What?

MARVALYN. Whatever he's teaching you. Tell him to stop. What he's teaching you … isn't something you wanna know.

STEVE. But I have to learn from him —

MARVALYN. Look: I was gonna be a nurse, so I know: You need to go to a doctor, and not have your brother read whatever it is he reads.

STEVE. But —

MARVALYN. You know what, I gotta go.

STEVE. *(Sits down on the bench.)* Right. You gotta go. You're —

you're leaving. I knew you would. That's what people do.

MARVALYN. No, I just have to — . I told you, Eric // doesn't like it if —

STEVE. Your boyfriend?

MARVALYN. Yeah, he doesn't like it if I'm down here longer than I said I'd be, and I've been down here longer than I said I'd be — *(On this line, Marvalyn picks up the ironing board. Then, as she goes to put it away, she accidentally swings it around and hits Steve in the head, just as she did at the beginning of the scene. Steve gets knocked off the bench.)*

STEVE. OW!

MARVALYN. Oh! I'm so sorry!

STEVE. OW!

MARVALYN. I'm so sorry!, are you all right? I can't believe I just did that to you again!

STEVE. OW!!

MARVALYN. *(She goes to help him; stops short.)* Wait — : What did you just say?

STEVE. *(As he rubs his head, he realizes what he just said. Beat. He looks at Marvalyn, tells her plainly:)* Ow. *(Music. Marvalyn and Steve just look at each other. Utter uncertainty. This is scary. And wonderful. But mostly a little scary — because who knows what's next. Lights fade. Transitional aurora. End of "This Hurts." After the lights have faded and "This Hurts" is over, we begin Scene Four, which is entitled …*

GETTING IT BACK

Music fades. We hear someone — Gayle — pounding on a door.

GAYLE. Lendall! *(More pounding.)* Lendall! *(More pounding.)* Lendall! *(Lights up on the living room of a small home in Almost, Maine. It is furnished with a comfortable chair and an end table. Lendall has been woken up. Maybe he was asleep in bed; maybe he was asleep in the chair. Either way, he's up now. He turns on the light, and goes to answer the door. Gayle continues to pound on the door.)*

LENDALL. Okay! Gayle! Shhh! I'm comin', I'm comin'!

GAYLE. Lendall!

LENDALL. Hey, hey, hey! Shh, come on, I'm comin'! *(Lendall exits stage left to answer the door.)*

GAYLE. *(Entering; blowing by him.)* Lendall —

LENDALL. *(Returning.)* What's the matter?, what's goin' on? *(Beat. Gayle is stewing.)* What?

GAYLE. *(She's been in a bit of a state, but she collects herself.)* I want it back.

LENDALL. What?

GAYLE. I want it back.

LENDALL. What?

GAYLE. All the love I gave to you?, I want it back.

LENDALL. What?

GAYLE. *Now.*

LENDALL. *(Little beat.)* I don't understand —

GAYLE. I've got yours in the car.

LENDALL. What?

GAYLE. All the love you gave to me?, I've got it in the car.

LENDALL. What are you talkin' about?

GAYLE. I don't want it anymore.

LENDALL. Why?

GAYLE. I've made a decision: We're done.

LENDALL. What?! —

GAYLE. We're done. I've decided. And, so, I've brought all the love you gave to me back to you. It's the right thing to do.

LENDALL. *(Bewildered.)* Um, I —

GAYLE. It's in the car.

LENDALL. You said. *(Beat. He's kind of paralyzed trying to figure this out.)*

GAYLE. *(Waiting for him to take some action and go get the love.)* I can get it *for* you, or … *you* can get it.

LENDALL. Well, I don't want it back. I don't need it —

GAYLE. Well, *I* don't want it! What am I supposed to do with all of it, now that I don't want it?

LENDALL. Well, I don't know …

GAYLE. Well, under the circumstances //, it doesn't seem right for me to keep it, so I'm gonna give it back. *(She leaves.)*

LENDALL. Under what circumstances? *(Calling to her.)* Gayle — what are — ? I don't understand what — … What are you doing?

GAYLE. *(From off.)* I told you. I'm getting all the love you gave to me, and I'm giving it back to you.

LENDALL. *(Calling to her.)* Well, I'm not sure I want it — whoa! Need help?

GAYLE. Nope. I got it. It's not heavy. *(She returns with an ENOR-MOUS bunch of HUGE red bags full of love. The bags should be filled with clothes or towels [for a little bit of weight and stability] and foam or pillow stuffing [for shape, and to keep them soundless]. She dumps the bags on the floor.)* Here you go.

LENDALL. *(Truly puzzled, referring to the bags of love.)* And this is … ?

GAYLE. *(Exiting.)* All the love you gave me, yeah.

LENDALL. Wow. *(Beat.)* That's a *lot*.

GAYLE. *(Returning with more bags of love.)* Yeah. *(She exits.)*

LENDALL. Whole lot.

GAYLE. Yeah. *(She returns with even more bags of love. There is now a GIGANTIC pile of love in Lendall's living room.)*

LENDALL. Wow. What the heck am I gonna do with all this? I mean … I don't know if I have room.

GAYLE. *(Upset.)* I'm sure you'll find a place for it *(I.e., another woman.)* … And now, I think it's only fair for you to give me mine back because … I want it back. *(Beat.)* All the love I gave to you?

LENDALL. Yeah?

GAYLE. I want it back. *(Beat.)* So go get it. *(Lendall doesn't move. He's probably trying to figure out what is happening and why it's happening.)* Lendall, go get it. *(Lendall still doesn't move.)* Please. *(Lendall still doesn't move.)* Now!!!

LENDALL. *(A little shaken; a little at a loss.)* Okay. *(Lendall exits. Gayle sits in the chair and waits. She's still in a state. Long beat. Lendall returns … with a teeny-tiny little bag — a little red pouch — and places it on a little table next to the chair. They look at the little bag. The little bag should be between Lendall and Gayle. And Gayle should be between the many bags of love and the little bag of love.)*

GAYLE. What is that?

LENDALL. *(It's obvious — it's exactly what she asked for.)* It's all the love you gave me.

GAYLE. That's — …? That is *not* — . There is no way — … That is *not* — . *(Mortified.)* Is that all I gave you?

LENDALL. It's all I could find …

GAYLE. Oh. Okay. *(Taking in the little bag … and then at all the big bags.)* Okay. *(And she's crying.)*

LENDALL. Gayle … What's goin' on, here?

GAYLE. I told you: We're done.

LENDALL. Why do you keep saying that?

GAYLE. Because —. *(This is hard to say, but has to be said.)*

Because when I asked you if you ever thought we were gonna get married — remember when I asked you that? *(Lendall doesn't seem to want to remember.)* In December? … It was snowing?

LENDALL. *(But he remembers.)* Yeah.

GAYLE. Yeah, well, when I asked you … *that*, you got so … *quiet*. And everybody said that that right there // shoulda told me everything.

LENDALL. Everybody *who?*

GAYLE. Everybody!

LENDALL. Who?

GAYLE. … Marvalyn >

LENDALL. *Marvalyn?!?* Marvalyn said that, like she's an expert?

GAYLE. said — yes, Marvalyn, yes, said that how quiet you got was all I needed to know, and she's right: You don't love me.

LENDALL. What — ? Gayle, no!

GAYLE. Shh! And I've been trying to fix that, I've tried to *make* you love me by giving you every bit of love I had, and now … I don't have any love for *me* left, and that's … that's not good for a person … and … that's why I want all the love I gave you back, because I wanna bring it with me.

LENDALL. Where are you going?

GAYLE. I need to get away from things.

LENDALL. What — ? What things?! There aren't any things in this town to get away from!

GAYLE. Yes there are: You!

LENDALL. Me?

GAYLE. Yes. *You* are the things in this town I need to get away from because I have to think and start over, and so: all the love I gave to you? I want it back, in case I need it. Because I can't very well go around giving *your* love — 'cause that's all I have right now, is the love *you* gave *me* — I can't very well go around giving *your* love to other guys, 'cause // that just doesn't seem right —

LENDALL. Other *guys?* There are other guys?!?

GAYLE. No, not yet, but I'm assuming there will be.

LENDALL. Gayle —

GAYLE. Shh!!! So I think — . I think that, since I know now that you're not ready to do what comes next for people who have been together for quite a long time *(I.e., get married.)*, I think we're gonna be done, >

LENDALL. Why? Gayle — !

GAYLE. and so, I think the best thing we can do, now, is just return the love we gave to each other, and call it … *(Taking in the bags — the pathetic one that contains the love she gave him, and the awesome several that contain the love he gave her.)* … even. *(It's not "even" at all.).* Oh, Jeezum Crow, is that really all the love I gave you, Lendall? I mean, I thought — . I mean, what kind of person am I if this is all the love I gave y — … No … n-n-no! *(Fiercely.)* I *know* I gave you more than that, Lendall, I *know* it! *(She thinks. Collects herself. New attack.)* Did you lose it?

LENDALL. What?!? // No, Gayle, no!

GAYLE. Did you *lose* it, Lendall? 'Cause I know I gave you more than that, and I think you're pulling something on me, and this is not a good time to be pulling something on me!

LENDALL. I'm not. Pulling something on you. I wouldn't do that to you … Just — I think — … Gosh — … *(Not mean; just at a loss.)* I think maybe you should just take what you came for, and I guess I'll see you later. *(This is pretty final. He exits into the rest of the house.)*

GAYLE. *(Realization of the finality; calls him, weakly.)* Lendall … Lendall … *(Now Gayle is at a loss. But this is what she wants. She looks at the little bag, takes it, and is about to leave. But curiosity stops her. She sits in the chair, opens the bag, and examines what's inside.)* Lendall!? What is this? What the heck is this, Lendall? This is *not* the love I gave you, Lendall, at least have the decency to give me back what — . Lendall, what is this?

LENDALL. *(From off.)* It's a ring, Gayle.

GAYLE. What?

LENDALL. *(Returning.)* It's a ring.

GAYLE. What? Well, what the — ? *(She takes what is in the bag out of the bag.)* This isn't — . This is *not* — … *(Realizes it's a ring box.)* Oh, Lendall, this is a ring! Is this a … *ring?* A ring that you give to someone you've been with for quite a long time if you want to let them know that you're ready for what comes next for people who have been together for quite a long time…?

LENDALL. Yup.

GAYLE. Oh … *(She opens the box, sees the ring.)* Oh! *(Beat.)* But … all the love I gave to you? Where is it?

LENDALL. It's right there, Gayle. *(Referring to the ring.)*

GAYLE. But —

LENDALL. It's right there.

GAYLE. But —

LENDALL. It *is*! That's it! Right there! There was so much of it

— you gave me so much, over the years —

GAYLE. *Eleven.*

LENDALL. — over the eleven // years —

GAYLE. *Eleven,* yeah.

LENDALL. — yeah, you gave me so much … that I didn't know what to do with it all. I had to put some in the garage, some in the shed. I asked my dad if he had any suggestions what to do with it all, and he said, "You got a ring yet?" I said, "No." And he said, "Get her one. It's time. When there's that much of that stuff comin' in, that's about the only place you can put it." *(Beat.)* He said it'd all fit. *(I.e., in the ring. Beat.)* And he was right. *(Beat. They look at the ring. Then, simply:)* That thing is a lot bigger than it looks … *(Beat.)* So, there it is. All the love you gave me. Just not in the same … form as when you gave it.

GAYLE. Yeah. *(Beat.)*

LENDALL. You still want it back?

GAYLE. Yes. I do.

LENDALL. Well, then … take it.

GAYLE. *(She takes the ring out of the box. Then, referring to all the bags of love:)* Can I keep all that?

LENDALL. It's yours.

GAYLE. Thank you. *(Lendall takes the ring, puts it on Gayle's finger. Music.)* Lendall — … You didn't have to get me a ring. That's not what I was asking —

LENDALL. Yes I did. It was time. And it's honorable.

GAYLE. Well … it's very beautiful. *(Beat.)* Lendall — … I'm so sorry. It's just — it's a Friday night, and I was sittin' home all by myself — we didn't even go out or anything, and I started thinkin' that that's just not right, and —

LENDALL. Shh. *(Into a kiss. And a hug. After a moment — still in the hug, and unbeknownst to Lendall — Gayle can't help herself but to take a good long look at that ring. Lights fade on Gayle and Lendall hugging and swaying — two small people in love, underneath a big, spectacular, star-lit northern night sky. Transitional aurora. End of "Getting It Back." End of Act One. Fade to black. Intermission. After the intermission, we move to what I'm calling the …*

INTERLOGUE

(NOTE: The "Interlogue" comes after the intermission.)
Music. Lights up on Pete, from the "Prologue." He is simply
waiting for Ginette. His snowball is on the bench next to him.
He looks offstage left, to where Ginette exited. He looks at his
snowball. He looks out. He bundles up against the cold. Lights
fade, and we begin ...

ACT TWO

with Scene Five, which is entitled ...

THEY FELL

Music fades. Lights up on Randy and Chad — these guys are one-hundred-percent "guy," two "Aroostook County boys" — hanging out in a potato field in Almost, Maine. They're prob-ably drinkin' some beers — Natural Lite, if you can get it. They're in mid-conversation.

CHAD. I believe you, I'm just sayin' —
RANDY. It was bad, Chad. *Bad.*
CHAD. I hear ya, b//ut —
RANDY. But you're not *listenin'*, // Chad: It was bad! >
CHAD. No, *you're* not listenin', 'cause >
RANDY. Real bad ...
CHAD. *(Topping Randy.)* I'm tryin' to tell you that I had a pretty bad time *myself!!!*
RANDY. *(Taking this in; then:)* No. There's no way! —
CHAD. It was pretty bad, Randy.
RANDY. Really.
CHAD. Yeah.
RANDY. Okay ... go. *[Let's hear it.]*
CHAD. *(This is a little painful.)* She — ... She said she didn't like the way I smelled.
RANDY. What?
CHAD. Sally told me she didn't like the way I smelled. Never has.
RANDY. *(Taking this in.)* Sally Dunleavy *(Say, "DUN-luv-ee.")* told you that she didn't // like the way — ...?
CHAD. Yeah.
RANDY. When?
CHAD. When I picked her up. She got in the truck — we were backin' outta her driveway — and all of a sudden, she starts breath-

in' hard and asked me to stop and she got outta the truck and said she was sorry, but she couldn't go out with me because she didn't like the way I smelled, never had!

RANDY. What?

CHAD. Said she thought she was gonna be able to overlook it, the way that I smelled, but that that wasn't gonna be possible after all, and she slammed the door on me and left me sittin' right there in her driveway.

RANDY. *(Taking this in.)* 'Cause she didn't like the way you smelled?

CHAD. Yeah.

RANDY. Well what kinda — ...? *(Beat.)* I don't mind the way you smell.

CHAD. Thanks.

RANDY. Jeez.

CHAD. Yeah ... *(Beat.)* Told you it was bad.

RANDY. More than bad, Chad. That's sad.

CHAD. Yeah. *(Beat.)* So, I'm guessin' I'm the big winner tonight, huh? So ... I get to pick tomorrow, and I pick bowlin'. We'll go bowlin', supper at the Snowmobile Club ... coupla beers at The Moose Paddy ... and just hang out.

RANDY. *(Looks at Chad. Beat.)* I didn't say you're the big winner, >

CHAD. What?

RANDY. did I say you're the big winner?

CHAD. No —

RANDY. No. All that's pretty sad, Chad, and bad, but you didn't win.

CHAD. What do you mean?

RANDY. You didn't win.

CHAD. You can beat bein' told you smelled bad?

RANDY. Yeah.

CHAD. Well, then ... *[Let's hear it.]*

RANDY. *(This is tough to share.)* Mine's face broke.

CHAD. What?

RANDY. Her face broke.

CHAD. *(Taking this in.)* Her — ?

RANDY. Only get one chance with a girl like Yvonne LaFrance, *("LaFrance" rhymes with "pants.")* and her face broke. *(Beat.)* Told you it was bad. *(Beat.)*

CHAD. How did her face break?

RANDY. When we were dancin'.

45

CHAD. *Dancin'? (These guys don't dance.)*

RANDY. Yup.

CHAD. Why were you *dancin'?*

RANDY. 'Cause that's what she wanted to do. On our date. So I took her. Took her dancin' down to the rec center. You pay, then you get a lesson, then you dance all night. They teach "together dancing," how to dance together, and we learned that thing where you throw the girl up and over, and, Yvonne — well, she's pretty small ... and I'm pretty strong. And I threw her up and over, and, well ... I threw her ... *over* ... over. *(Beat.)* And she landed on her face. *(Beat.)* And it broke. *(Beat.)* Had to take her to the emergency room. *(Long beat. Then, finally:)*

CHAD. That's a drive.

RANDY. Thirty-eight miles.

CHAD. Yup. *(Beat.)*

RANDY. *(Disgusted.)* And she cried.

CHAD. Hate that.

RANDY. Whole way. *(Beat.)* Then had me call her old boyfriend to come get her.

CHAD. Ooh.

RANDY. He did. Asked me to "please leave." *(Beat.)* He's small as she is. *(They laugh. Beat. Chad laughs.)* What?

CHAD. That's just — pretty bad.

RANDY. Yup.

CHAD. And sad.

RANDY. Yup.

CHAD. So ... I guess you win.

RANDY. Yup!

CHAD. That right there might make you the big winner of all time!

RANDY. Yup!

CHAD. "Baddest-date-guy" of all time!

RANDY. Yup!

CHAD. Congratulations!

RANDY. Thank you!

CHAD. So what do you pick tomorrow?

RANDY. Bowlin'. Supper at the Snowmobile Club. Coupla beers at the Moose Paddy. Hang out.

CHAD. Good. *(Beat. They drink their beers, and crush the cans, and shoot them into crates or an offstage abandoned potato barrel, maybe. Everything settles. Beat. Chad laughs.)*

RANDY. What?

CHAD. *(Sitting.)* I don't know. Just sometimes ... I don't know why I bother goin' "out." I don't like it, Randy. I hate it. I hate goin' out on these dates. I mean, why do I wanna spend my Friday night with some girl I might *maybe* like, when I could be spendin' it hangin' out with someone I *know* I like, like you, you know?
RANDY. Yeah.
CHAD. I mean ... that was rough tonight. In the middle of Sally tellin' me how she didn't like the way I smelled ... I got real sad, >
RANDY. Aw, buddy ...
CHAD. and all I could think about was how not much in this world makes me feel good or makes much sense anymore, and I got really scared, 'cause there's gotta be something that makes you feel good or at least makes sense in this world, or what's the point, right? But then I kinda came out of bein' sad, and actually felt okay, 'cause I realized that there *is* one thing in this world that makes me feel really good and that *does* make sense, and it's you. *(Everything stops. Chad isn't quite sure what he has just said. Randy isn't quite sure what he has just heard. Long, long beat of these guys sorting out what was just said and heard.)*
RANDY. *(Escaping the discomfort.)* Well, I'm gonna head. *(He starts to leave.)* >
CHAD. Yeah ...
RANDY. *(Deflecting throughout the following.)* I gotta work in the mornin' ...
CHAD. Well, I'm just supervisin' first shift at the mill, so I can pick you up anytime after three —
RANDY. Oh, I don't know, Chad: Me and Lendall, we got a long day tomorrow — we're still catchin' up, fixin' roofs from all the snow in December, // gotta do Marvalyn and Eric's, and —
CHAD. Well, four // or five? Or six or seven?
RANDY. Prob'ly busy all day, I don't know when we'll be // done.
CHAD. Well, you just // say when —
RANDY. I don't know, I don't know!, so, >
CHAD. Well —
RANDY. *(Putting a stop to this — he wants outta there.)* hey-HEY!! I'll see ya later! *(He leaves.)*
CHAD: Yeah. Yeah-yeah-yeah ... *(Chad watches Randy go. Then:)* Hey, Randy! — *(Suddenly, Chad completely falls down on the ground. Maybe it's more of a crumple to the ground. Love is, after all, often described as making people weak in the knees.)*
RANDY. *(Rushing back, seeing Chad on the ground.)* Whoa! Chad!

47

You okay?

CHAD. Yeah …

RANDY. What the — … Here … *(Helps Chad up.)*

CHAD. Thanks. Umm …

RANDY. What was that? You okay? What just happened there?

CHAD. *(Trying to figure this out.)* Umm … I just fell …

RANDY. Well, I figured that out …

CHAD. No — … I just — . *(Beat.)* I think I just … fell in love with you there, Randy. *(Beat. Randy is silent. What has Chad just said? What has Randy just heard? Chad looks at Randy, then suddenly and completely falls down again.)*

RANDY/CHAD. Chad! / Whoa …

CHAD. *(On the ground.)* Yup. That's what that was. *(Getting up.)* Me falling in love with you … *(He looks at Randy, and falls down again, suddenly and completely.)*

RANDY. Chad: What are you doin'? Come on, get up! *(Randy gets Chad up, roughly.)*

CHAD. No-no-no, Randy — *(Chad looks at Randy and immediately falls down again.)*

RANDY. *(Fiercely.)* Would you cut that out?!?

CHAD. *(Fiercely, right back, and from the ground.)* Well, I can't help it!! It just kinda came over me!! I've fallen in love with ya, here!!

RANDY. *(Takes this in. Confused, scared. Long beat. Then:)* Chad: I'm your best buddy in the whole world … and I don't quite know what you're doin' or what you're goin' on about … but *(Angry.)* — what the heck is your problem?!? What the heck are you doin'?!? Jeezum Crow, you're my best friend, >

CHAD. Yeah —

RANDY. and that's — … That's a thing you don't mess with. And you messed with it. And you don't *do* that. *(He starts to go, but stops — he's not done yet.)* 'Cause, you know somethin', you're about the only thing that feels really good and makes sense in this world to me, too, and then you go and foul it up, by doin' *this (I.e., falling down.)* and tellin' me *that (I.e., that you're in love with me.)*, and now it just doesn't make any sense at all. And it doesn't feel good. *(Starts to go again, but stops — he's still not done yet.)* You've done a real number on a good thing, here, buddy, 'cause we're friends, and there's a line when you're friends that you can't cross. And you crossed it! *(Little beat. And then, Randy, who is now on the opposite side of the stage from Chad, suddenly and completely falls down. Beat.*

48

Randy and Chad look at each other. A moment of realization. This is about as scary — and wonderful — as it gets. Now — the guys are far away from each other, and all they want to do is get to each other, so they go to get up — in order to get to each other — but suddenly and completely fall down. This is weird. They scramble to get up again, to see if they can "beat" the fall, but they fall down again. They desperately want to get to each other, so — in a bit of a frenzy, to try to "beat" the falls — they try to get up, they fall down; they get up, they fall down; they get up, they fall down; they get up, they fall down; they get up, they fall down. The falling frenzy settles ... and Randy and Chad are no closer to each other than they were when they started. Beat. Music. They just look at each other. It's all scary and thrilling and unknown. It's going to be wonderful. Just not quite yet. Lights fade. Transitional aurora. End of "They Fell." After the lights have faded and "They Fell" is over, we begin Scene Six, which is entitled ...

WHERE IT WENT

Music fades. Lights up on Phil and Marci, who have just been ice-skating on Echo Pond in Almost, Maine. They are undoing their skates, putting on their boots/shoes. Phil has hockey skates; Marci has figure skates. Marci has one shoe on, one skate on. Note: Marci should be wearing a winter shoe — like an L.L. Bean hunting shoe, or a suede-like winter shoe — not a boot. Beat.

PHIL. It still feels like you're mad.
MARCI. *(Undoing her skate.)* I'm not mad, // I just said I wish >
PHIL. But you were, you *are,* >
MARCI. you'd pay more attention lately.
PHIL. you're mad.
MARCI. I'm not mad! I was having fun, I thought. I had fun tonight. Did you?
PHIL. Yeah.
MARCI. Good. *(Smiles, continues to undo her skates; is puzzled by something. Beat.)*
PHIL. *(Continuing his defense.)* I mean, Chad called me in to the

mill, I had to work.

MARCI. *(Looking for something.)* I'm not mad at you, Phil, you had to work, // I get it.

PHIL. I did!

MARCI. *(Now actively looking for something.)* Phil, where's my shoe?

PHIL. What?

MARCI. Where's my shoe, I can't find it.

PHIL. Well, it's gotta be here ...

MARCI. Where is it?!? *(They look for her shoe. Beat.)* Is this you being funny?

PHIL. No.

MARCI. 'Cause it's not funny. >

PHIL. I —

MARCI. It's cold out here!

PHIL. Well, you're the one that wanted to go skating!

MARCI. Phil!

PHIL. *(Angry — a bit of an explosion.)* We'll find it! It's gotta be here! *(Beat.)*

MARCI. I'm not mad. I was never mad. *(Re-lacing her skate — too cold for stocking feet. Beat.)* I was disappointed. But now I'm // done.

PHIL. Marce! —

MARCI. I had fun tonight! Skating! I thought it would be fun!, >

PHIL. It *was* ...

MARCI. forget all the ... stuff. Get us away from the kids, get us back to where we used to be. We went skating ... first time you kissed me, on a Friday night just like this one. 'Member? Right here ... *(She touches Phil in some way — maybe rubs his back.)* Echo Pond —

PHIL. *(Subtly/subconsciously shaking off Marci's touch.)* I know where we are, where the heck is your shoe? *(Going off to look for it.)* Maybe it's — maybe it's in the car. Did you — ... Where'd you put your skates on, out here or in the car? *(We hear him open the doors and trunk of the car.)*

MARCI. *(Dealing with the fact that Phil shrugged her off.)* I put them on with you. Right here. *(Beat. She looks to the sky for answers.)*

PHIL. *(Returning.)* Well, it's // not in the car —

MARCI. *(She sees a shooting star.)* Oh-oh-oh!!! Shooting star, shooting star! *(She closes her eyes, and makes a wish.)*

50

PHIL. Wha — // Where, where?!? *(He looks for it.)*
MARCI. *(Eyes closed.)* Shh!! I'm wishing, I'm wishing!
PHIL. *(Keeps looking, and then:)* Oh, I missed it.
MARCI. *(Just looks at him.)* Yeah, you did.
PHIL. What's that supposed to mean?
MARCI. *(Finishes re-lacing her skate, eventually gets up to look for her shoe.)* Nothin' — it's just ... not really all that surprising >
PHIL. What?
MARCI. that you didn't see it.
PHIL. What?
MARCI. The shooting star.
PHIL. Why?
MARCI. You don't pay attention, Phil. *(Beat.)*
PHIL. See, when you say things like that, I feel like you're still mad.
MARCI. I'm not.
PHIL. Marce —
MARCI. I wasn't mad, *(Frustrated about a lot more than her missing shoe.)* WHERE is my *shoe?!?!* Gosh, maybe it *is* in the car. *(Going offstage, to the car, to look for her other shoe.)* I mean, >
PHIL. It's not in the car ...
MARCI. I have one shoe on already. *(From off.)* I *know* I didn't put my skates on in the car, 'cause the shoe I have on was out there. I changed out there, didn't I? With you? Phil? *(Phil doesn't answer. He is trying to sort out what's going with him, his wife. He's sad. From off:)* Phil? I put my shoes right next to yours, after we put our skates on, but it's not ... there ... This is the weirdest thing. *(Returning.)* It's not in the car, I mean, I'm not gonna put one skate on in the car, the other one on out here — *(Sees how sad Phil is.)* What's wrong?
PHIL. *(Covering.)* Huh? Oh. I'm ... making a wish of my own. On a regular one.
MARCI. Oh.
PHIL. Wanna wish on it with me?
MARCI. Yeah. Yeah, that'd be nice. Which one?
PHIL. Umm ... see Hedgehog Mountain?
MARCI. Uh-huh.
PHIL. Straight up, right above it.
MARCI. The bright one?
PHIL. Yeah.
MARCI. That one?

PHIL. Yeah.

MARCI. Right there?

PHIL. Yeah.

MARCI. Phil:

PHIL. Yeah?

MARCI. That's a planet.

PHIL. What?

MARCI. That's a planet. You're wishing on a planet.

PHIL. That's a — ?

MARCI. Yeah, >

PHIL. Well, how do you know?

MARCI. and it's *(She sings.)* " … when you wish upon a *star*," not " … when you wish upon a *planet* // or *Saturn —* "

PHIL. I know, I know! How do you know?

MARCI. Said on the weather, Phil. Saturn's the brightest object in the sky this month. It'll be sitting right above Hedgehog Mountain over the next bunch of weeks. They've been sayin' it on the weather all week. And your wish is never gonna come true if you're wishing on a planet.

PHIL. Well —

MARCI. You gotta pay attention.

PHIL. Why do you keep sayin' that?

MARCI. What?

PHIL. That I gotta pay attention?

MARCI. 'Cause you don't.

PHIL. What are you talkin' about? —

MARCI. Phil: Happy Anniversary. *(Beat.)*

PHIL. Huh?

MARCI. Happy Anniversary. That's what I'm talkin' about. *(Beat.)*

PHIL. I'm — . *(Can't quite say he's sorry. Beat. Then, instead of apologizing:)* I knew you were mad.

MARCI. I'm not mad, // Phil!

PHIL. You're mad at me, and pretty soon, outta nowhere, it's gonna get ugly. >

MARCI. Phil, I'm not mad, I'm —

PHIL. I mean, Marce: I'm *sorry!!* I know I missed some things, but I gotta work! I gotta take a double when Chad needs me at the mill! He's helpin' me — *us* — out, you know, // offering me the overtime!

MARCI. I know, I know —

PHIL. No, you *don't* know: Me workin' is for *us*, and the kids, and it's a lot sometimes, and it messes me up!

MARCI. Phil! I'm not mad about you workin'. You gotta work. I understand that. What I don't understand is why I'm lonely, Phil. I got a husband and a coupla great kids. And I'm lonely. *(Beat.)* You just — ... you don't pay attention anymore. You go away. And I don't know where you go, but you go somewhere where you can't pay attention and you forget your son's first hockey game and // you forget Missy's birthday and >

PHIL. Hockey equipment costs money!

MARCI. you forget your *anniversary!* I mean, I brought you here hoping you'd remember about us. But you didn't. And that makes me so mad I don't know what to do anymore ... *(Beat.)*

PHIL. You *lie.*

MARCI. What?

PHIL. You lie so bad.

MARCI. What?

PHIL. You're mad at me. But you don't *tell* me — even when I ask you over and over —

MARCI. Because *you* wouldn't // pay attention if I *did* tell you —

PHIL. No! No! No! Because *you* don't know how to tell me what you feel like about me, so I never know where I am, where I stand! Maybe that's why I go away! So I can know where I am for a second! And you know what, it's lonely there too, where I go. And you sent me there. You went away a long time before I did. And now all's you do is lie.

MARCI. I don't lie!

PHIL. *(Furious.)* Yes you do! You say you're not mad, but you're mad! You say you have fun, but you didn't! You didn't have fun tonight, did you?

MARCI. No.

PHIL. But you kept sayin' you did.

MARCI. I didn't. I didn't have fun, Phil. I don't have fun with you anymore. *(Beat.)* Did you?

PHIL. No. I had a rotten, lousy time. *(Beat.)*

MARCI. Well, then ... *(Little beat.)* what are we doin'? What are we waiting for? *(Beat. And then ... a shoe that looks exactly like Marci's other shoe drops from the sky, right between Marci and Phil. Beat. Marci and Phil survey the sky, trying to figure out what just happened. Music. Phil retrieves the shoe and gives it to Marci, who puts it on. Marci gets up. She then takes the car keys out of her pocket, exits, and we hear her start the car and drive away. Phil is alone. A shooting star cuts across the night sky on the field of stars. Phil sees it. Lights*

53

fade. Transitional aurora. End of "Where It Went." After the lights have faded and "Where It Went" is over, we begin Scene Seven, which is entitled ...

STORY OF HOPE

Music fades. Sound of a car approaching, idling. A car door opens, then closes. Sound of car leaving. Sound of fancy-shoed footsteps in snow approaching. Doorbell. Lights up on a woman standing on the front porch of a small home in Almost, Maine. She carries a suitcase and a purse. Note: The actor playing the man must be short or thin. This is crucial to the magic of the story. "Story of Hope" is a story of loss, and a physical manifestation of loss in the man is key — lost height [again, this is best!], lost weight — because this man is literally half the man he used to be because he has lost so much hope. You'll be surprised by how magical and heartbreaking and funny this scene is when the physical manifestation of the man's loss is crystal clear.

MAN. *(From off.)* Just a minute ... *(The lights come on in the house; then a porch light comes on. A man who is not the man he used to be answers the door a bit cautiously. Nine o'clock at night is, after all, the middle of the night. He's in pajamas and a bathrobe. He enters and stops cold. He knows this woman.)*
WOMAN. *(Fast and furious; so absorbed by what she has to say and by what she has come to do, that she really doesn't take in/look at the man.)* I know this isn't going to be very easy, but I was just out there all alone in the world, and I got so scared, because all I could think about was how I had no place in this world, but then I just outta nowhere realized that there was one place in this world that I did have, and that was with you, so I flew and I took a taxi to get to you, I just had to come see you, *(Finally really looking at him.)* thank God you're — ... *(The man is not who she thought he'd be.)* Oh — ... Wait — ... I'm sorry. You're not — ... I'm — ... *(Checking to make sure she's at the right place.)* This is the house — ... I'm so sorry — ... Does Daniel Harding live here?, I'm looking for Daniel Harding.

MAN. You're // looking for —

WOMAN. Looking for Daniel Harding, yeah. He *lives* here. I thought. But … *(Off the man's confused state, realizing.)* … ooooh … he doesn't, does he? Oooh. I am so sorry. *(The woman gathers her bags, preparing to leave.)* I'm so embarrassed. "Who is this woman and what is she doing here?" *(Beat.)* I just honestly thought he'd be here. I always thought he'd be here. Always. *(Beat.)* Do you know him? Big guy, big tall guy. Played basketball, all-Eastern Maine, center? *Strong.* Do you know him? // Hockey, too? > *(NOTE: If the actor playing the man is not short, but thin or average, please use these lines:* Do you know him? Big guy, big strong guy. Wrestled? Heavyweight? All-Eastern Maine? *Strong?* Do you know him? // Played hockey, too? >)

MAN. Well … —

WOMAN. Oh, don't even answer that. That was — . I know that's a horrible question to ask a person who lives in a small town, as if everybody in small towns knows everybody else, agh!, can't believe I asked that. I don't live here anymore, but when I did, I hated it when people assumed I knew everybody in town just because it was small. It was worse than when they'd ask if we had " … plumbing way up there?," 'cause, you know, people in small towns really don't know each other any better than in big towns, you know that? I mean, you know who you know, and you don't know who you don't know, just like anywhere else. *(Beat.)* I'm so sorry to have bothered you. I was just so sure — . When his parents passed away, he kept the house, I heard. He lived here. He stayed here, I thought. He was one of the ones who stayed. *(Beat.)* I didn't stay. I went away.

MAN. Most people do.

WOMAN. Yeah. And I guess he did too. I never thought he would. I guess I lost track … You gotta hold onto people or you lose 'em. Wish there was something you could keep 'em in for when you need 'em … *(Trying to make light, she "looks for him," and "finds him" in her purse.)* Oh, there he is, perfect! *(She laughs. Not much of a response from the man. Beat. She starts to go; stops.)* Boy it's cold. I forgot.

MAN. Yeah. *(Beat.)*

WOMAN. *(Starts to go. Stops.)* I can't *believe* — … I took a taxi here. From Bangor. *(Say, "BANG-gore." Bangor is Maine's third largest city, pop. 31,000. It is one hundred and sixty-three miles south of Almost, Maine.)* To see him.

MAN. *(Beat. She took a taxi one hundred and sixty-three miles.)* That's far.

WOMAN. Yeah.

MAN. That's a hundred and sixty-three miles.

WOMAN. Yeah. This place is a little farther away from things than I remember.

MAN. Why did you do that?

WOMAN. Because I could only fly as close as Bangor and I needed to get to him as fast as I could.

MAN. Why?

WOMAN. Because I want to answer a question he asked me.

MAN. Oh?

WOMAN. The last time I saw him, he asked me a very important question and I didn't answer it, and that's just not a very nice thing to do to a person.

MAN. Well, that's bein' a little hard on yourself, don't you th//ink?

WOMAN. He asked me to marry him.

MAN. Oh. *(Beat.)* And you …

WOMAN. Didn't answer him. No. *(The man whistles.)* Yeah. And that's why I'm here. To answer him. *(Beat. Then, realizing she probably ought to defend herself.)* I mean, I didn't answer him in the first place because I didn't *have* an answer at the time. I mean, I was going to *college*, and then … the *night* before I'm about to go off into the world to do what I hope and dream, he asks me, "Will you marry me?" I mean, come on! I was leaving in the morning … What was I supposed to do?

MAN. I don't know.

WOMAN. *(Defending herself.)* I mean, I *told* him I'd have to think about it, that I'd think it over overnight and that I'd be back before the sun came up with an answer. And then I left. Left him standing right … *(Where the man is standing.)* … there … and then … I didn't make it back with an answer before the sun came up or … at all.

MAN. That sounds like an answer to me.

WOMAN. No! That wasn't my answer! I just … went off into the world, and that's not an answer, and I think — … *(Little beat.)*

MAN. What?

WOMAN. I think he thought I'd say, "Yes."

MAN. Well, a guy's probably not gonna ask a girl that question unless he thinks she's gonna say, "Yes."

WOMAN. I know, and … I'm afraid he probably waited up all night, hoping for me to come by, and I just want to tell him that I know now that you just can't do a thing like not answer a question like the one he asked me, you can't do that to a person. Especially to someone you love.

MAN. *(Taking this in.)* You loved him?

WOMAN. Well — . I don't know if — . I mean, we were kids. *(She considers. Then, honest and true:)* Yes. I did. I do. *(Beat.)* I feel like I dashed his hopes and dreams.

MAN. *(This speech is not an attack. It's more of a rumination — one that doesn't do much to make the woman feel better.)* Oh, come on. You give yourself too much credit. He was young. That's all you need to get your hopes dashed: Be young. And everybody starts out young, so … everybody gets their hopes dashed, and besides … I don't think you really *dashed* his hopes. 'Cause if you *dash* somebody's hopes — well that's … kind of a nice way to let 'em down, 'cause it *hurts* … but it's quick. If you'd have said, "No," *that* woulda been "dashing his hopes." *(Beat. Maybe a little pointed here.)* But you didn't say, "No." You said nothin'. You just didn't answer him. At all. And that's … killin' hope the long, slow, painful way, 'cause it's still there just hangin' on, never really goes away. And that's … kinda like givin' somebody a little less air to breathe every day. Till they die.

WOMAN. *(Taking in this very unhelpful information.)* Yeah … *(Beat. Then, at a loss:)* Well … thank you.

MAN. For what?

WOMAN. *(Considers; then, honestly:)* I don't know. *(She starts to leave.)*

MAN. *(After a beat.)* Goodbye, Hope.

HOPE. Goodbye. *(Stopping.)* Agh!, I'm so … sorry to have bothered you … It's just, I was all alone out there in the world with no place in it, and I realized what I'd done to him, to Danny, and that with him was my place in the world — … Wait … *(Realization.)* You called me Hope. How did you know my name? *(The man gently presents himself — maybe removes his glasses — and the woman recognizes him: He's Daniel Harding.)* Danny?!?

DANIEL. Hello, Hope.

HOPE. *(In a bit of a spin.)* Danny … I didn't // rec — >

DANIEL. I know.

HOPE. I didn't // rec — >

DANIEL. I know.

HOPE. I didn't even // recognize you!

DANIEL. I know.

HOPE. You're so …

DANIEL. I know.

HOPE. … small.

DANIEL. Yeah. I, uh, lost a lotta hope. That'll do a number on you. *(Long beat. They don't hug. Or greet each other physically. It should be awful.)*

HOPE. Danny: I'm so sorry I // never —

DANIEL. Shh ... It's okay. 'Cause, you know somethin'? You're early.

HOPE. What?

DANIEL. You're early! You said you'd be back with an answer to my question before the sun came up, and Jeezum Crow, the sun's not even close to being up yet! It only went down a few hours ago. Look how early you are! That's good of you. *(Beat. They enjoy his goodness.)* So, a taxi all the way from Bangor.

HOPE. Yup.

DANIEL. To tell me...? *(Hope is about to say, "Yes," when she is interrupted by:)*

SUZETTE. *(From off.)* Honey? Dan? Hon? Who's there?

DANIEL. *(Beat.)* Just somebody ... needs directions.

SUZETTE. It's awful late for directions.

DANIEL. Yeah — Suzette, listen ... *(Beat.)* ... I'll be right in.

SUZETTE. Okay ... *(Beat.)*

DANIEL. I — ...

HOPE. What?

DANIEL. *(Simple — not precious.)* I hope you find it, Hope. Your place in this world. *(Beat.)* Bye.

HOPE. Goodbye, Danny. *(Danny goes inside. Hope lingers — she is at a loss. Finally — after all these years — she answers Danny. She knows he won't hear her. She knows it wouldn't matter if he did. But she answers him anyway.)* Yes. *(Beat. Then, smaller and to herself:)* Yes. *(Music. Hope starts to go; she turns back. The porch light goes out. Lights fade. Transitional aurora. End of "Story of Hope." As the lights fade, and "Story of Hope" is over, we begin Scene Eight, which is entitled ...*

SEEING THE THING

Music fades. Sound of two snowmobiles approaching and parking. The lights from their headlights can be seen offstage as they approach. Lights up on the winterized porch of a small shack, in the middle of nowhere — but still within the "town" limits of Almost, Maine. Rhonda and Dave — the snowmobilers — enter, kicking the snow off their boots. They are carrying their snowmobile helmets and are dressed in layer upon layer upon layer of snowmobile/winter clothing. Dave has a present — a wrapped painting — behind his back. Beat.

RHONDA. *(She is not comfortable with having Dave in her house. This is a first.)* Okay. This is it. You're in. You're inside.

DAVE. This is the porch. *(He'd like to go further inside.)*

RHONDA. It's winterized. *(This is as far as he's getting. Beat.)* So, Dave: *What?!* What do you gotta do in here that you couldn't do outside?

DAVE. Well, I got somethin', here, for ya, here. *(He presents his wrapped gift, creating "awkward present beat #1.")*

RHONDA. What's this?

DAVE. It's — . It's — . It's — . *(Changing the subject, explosively dispelling the tension.)* Boy, that was fun tonight, Rhonda! >

RHONDA. Yeah, was!

DAVE. I mean, twenty miles out there, >

RHONDA. Yeah!

DAVE. beans and franks at the Snowmobile Club, >

RHONDA. Yeah!

DAVE. twenty miles back, coupla beers at The Moose Paddy!

RHONDA. Awesome!

DAVE. Yeah, and, boy, you flew on your new sled, // man!

RHONDA. It's a Polaris *(Say, "pull-AIR-iss." Polaris is a brand of snowmobile.)*, man!

DAVE. I know, and you whupped *("Whupped" sounds like "looked" or "cooked.")* my butt!

RHONDA. Yeah! That's what you get for ridin' an Arctic Cat: *(Arctic Cat is a competing brand of snowmobile.)* Ya get yer butt whupped! And I whupped it!

DAVE. I know!

RHONDA. Whupped your butt!

DAVE. I know!

RHONDA. Whupped it!

DAVE. I know!

RHONDA. Whupped your butt, Arctic Cat-Man!!

DAVE. I know, I know, I'm not sayin' ya didn't!

RHONDA. *(Settling down.)* That was fun. *(Beat. Everything stops*

59

again. They look at the wrapped gift. Call this "awkward present beat #2.")

DAVE. So, this is, um ... Well, we been ... together now —

RHONDA. *(Scoffing.) Together?*

DAVE. Well —

RHONDA. *Together?!?* What are you *talkin'* about, "together"???

DAVE. Well, we been friends for quite a few years // now, and, well —

RHONDA. You gettin' all girl on me?

DAVE. — *shh!* — and, and, and — ... And, here. *(He presents her with his gift.)*

RHONDA. *(These two don't give each other presents.)* What are you doin' here, bud?

DAVE. Open it.

RHONDA. "Together." Hmm. I don't know about this ...

DAVE. Just open it.

RHONDA. *(She opens the present downstage center. The present — a wrapped canvas painting — must be opened in such a way that the audience cannot see what it is. Once Rhonda opens it, she props the painting up against a crate — still so that the audience can't see it. She has no idea what it is a painting is of. Beat.)* What is it?

DAVE. What do you mean, what is it? Can't you ... see what // it is —

RHONDA. It's a picture ...

DAVE. Yeah ...

RHONDA. A paintin'.

DAVE. Yeah.

RHONDA. Where'd you get this? It looks homemade.

DAVE. What do you mean, it looks homemade?

RHONDA. Looks like someone really painted it.

DAVE. Well, someone really *did* paint it.

RHONDA. *(Realizing.)* Did you paint this?

DAVE. Yeah.

RHONDA. For me?

DAVE. Yeah.

RHONDA. Oh ... *(She has no idea what it is, what to make of it.)* Why?!?

DAVE. Well — ... *(He painted it 'cause he thinks the whole world of her.)*

RHONDA. I mean ... thank you! // Thank you, thanks, yeah.

DAVE. There you go!, that's what people say!, there you go! You're welcome.

RHONDA. *(Sitting in chair, center, staring at her painting.)* So, Dave … I didn't know you *painted.*

DAVE. Yeah. This is — … *(Turns his painting right side up — Rhonda propped it up wrong. Then:)* I'm takin' adult ed art. At nights. Merle Haslem over at the high school's teachin' it, it's real good. And this is my version of one of those stare-at-it-until-you-see-the-thing things. Ever seen one of these? Some of the old painters did it with dots. They called it — … *(Searches, but can't quite come up with "pointillism.")* somethin' … but I did it with a buncha little blocks of colors, see, and if you just look at the blocks of colors, it's just colors, but if you step back and look at the whole thing, it's not just little blocks of colors, it's a picture of something.

RHONDA. Picture of what?

DAVE. I'm not gonna tell you, you have to figure it out.

RHONDA. Oh, come on, Dave!

DAVE. No, it takes a little time, it can be a little frustrating.

RHONDA. Well, why would you give me somethin' that's gonna *frustrate?!?*

DAVE. No, no, no, I just mean you gotta not *try* to look for anything, that's what'll frustrate you. You gotta just *kinda* look at it, so it doesn't *know* you're lookin' at it.

RHONDA. What're you talkin' about?

DAVE. You gotta trick it! *(Demonstrates "tricking it" — steals glances at it as he walks by it.)* Trick it! *(More demonstrations.)* See? Trick it, trick it! Gotta not let it know. And hopefully you'll eventually see what it is. It's a common thing, it's somethin' everybody knows. *(Rhonda tries "trickin' it" a few times, like Dave did. This "trickin' it" business should be pretty darn funny.)* There ya go, there ya go!

RHONDA. *(Gives up on "trickin' it.")* This is stupid. I don't see anything.

DAVE. No, you were doin' good!

RHONDA. Dave!

DAVE. All right, all right, then, do this: Do what you usually do around the house at night, and check it out real casual-like, *(Demonstrating.)* and —

RHONDA. I usually have a Bud and talk to you on the phone.

DAVE. Well, do that. Where's the kitchen? *(Starting into the house.)* // I'll get you a Bud, and you can talk to me —

RHONDA. *(Stopping him — she doesn't want him going inside.)* N-n-n-n-no! >

DAVE. What?

RHONDA. I'm outta Bud. Only got Natty Lite.

DAVE. *(Starting back into the house.)* All right, I'll get you a Natty Lite, // and you can have your beer and talk to me —

RHONDA. *(Stopping him.)* N-n-no!

DAVE. Why not? Come on, let's go inside and get us a coupla beers! >

RHONDA. No! *(Back to the painting.)* We gotta trick this thing, right? See? I'm trickin' it, I'm trickin' it! Trickin' it, I'm trickin' it!

DAVE. It's what people who've known each other for a long time do. *Come on!! HEY!!! (Stopping her "trickin' it" routine.)* Quit it!! How many years I know ya, I come all the way out here every Friday night, and I never been inside your house for beers?! That's unnatural. It's unnatural, // Rhonda! So let's do what's the *natural* thing to do and go inside and have some beers — !

RHONDA. I don't care what it is, I gotta trick this thing. Hey! Hey-hey-hey, *DAVE!!* Quit runnin' your *suck!!* I gotta look. At this thing. *(She sits; stares straight at the painting, which frustrates Dave.)*

DAVE. You're doin' it wrong!

RHONDA. Shh!

DAVE. You gotta trick it, you gotta trick it! —

RHONDA. Hey-hey-hey!, okay, okay!! I got somethin'!

DAVE. Yeah?

RHONDA. Yeah! Yeah-yeah-yeah: Roadkill.

DAVE. What?

RHONDA. Roadkill. Dead raccoon in the middle of the road.

DAVE. What? No! That's not what it is! —

RHONDA. Okay, deer. Dead bloody deer // in the middle of the road —

DAVE. What?!? No!! Rhonda! It's not // a dead deer in the middle of the road!!

RHODA: Okay, moose. >

DAVE. What?

RHONDA. Dead bloody moose in the middle of the road.

DAVE. *RHONDA!!!* No!!! No!!! That's not somethin' I'd wanna *paint!!!* // That's not even close to what it is! Dead *moose?!?* Come on!!!

RHONDA. Well, that's what I see, I don't know what it is, don't get *mad,* Jeezum Crow!

DAVE. You don't see what it is?!?

RHONDA. No.

DAVE. Well, can I give you a hint?

RHONDA. Yeah! *(Dave kisses her right on the mouth. That's the hint. She immediately gets up/pulls away. Then, angry/flustered:)* What are you doin'?!? *(Little beat.)* What was that?!? Why did you do that?!?

DAVE. 'Cause I was giving you a hint — …

RHONDA. Don't ever do that again. *Ever!* And GET OUTTA HERE!!! *(She storms off into the house. Beat.)*

DAVE. *(Gathering his things; to himself:)* Jeezum Crow … *(He starts to go; stops; then, exploding:)* HEY, RHONDA!!

RHONDA. What?

DAVE. *You really are what they say!!*

RHONDA. What? What do they say?

DAVE. *That you're a little hung up, there!!!*

RHONDA. *(Reentering forcefully.)* Who says that?!?

DAVE. *(Retreating — she's tough.)* Everybody.

RHONDA. *(Continuing to advance.)* Everybody who?

DAVE. *(Retreating.)* Everybody, Rhonda. It's what people in town say …

RHONDA. When?

DAVE. When they're *talkin'!* They say that you're a little hung up, there, so I gotta be a little persistent, there, they say, and they were right!

RHONDA. Who says?

DAVE. *(Tough question to answer, 'cause these are their best buds.)* Suzette.

RHONDA. *Suzette?*

DAVE. Yeah, and Dan …

RHONDA. *(Disbelief.)* Suzette and Dan *Harding* say that I'm a little hung up, there, and that you gotta be a little persistent there…???

DAVE. Yeah.

RHONDA. Well, who else?

DAVE. Marci …

RHONDA. *Marci?!?*

DAVE. Yeah, and Phil, // and — >

RHONDA. Marci and *Phil?!?* —

DAVE. — yeah — and Randy and Chad, and >

RHONDA. *Randy and Chad?!?* —

DAVE. Lendall and Gayle, and >

RHONDA. *Gayle?* —

63

DAVE. Marvalyn and Eric, and >

RHONDA. Marvalyn…?

DAVE. and Jimmy, and Sandrine, and East, and >

RHONDA. *East??*

DAVE. that's just to name a few …

RHONDA. *(Deeply, deeply hurt.)* Well, why would they — …? I love those guys. I'm good to those guys. Why would they say that about me? That's talkin' about me. That's mean.

DAVE. No — . I don't think they're bein' mean, Rhonda. I think they said that *(I.e., that you're a little hung up there.)* to me about you to kinda warn me what I was gettin' myself into with you. 'Cause they like you. And me. Us. They're rootin' for us, Rhonda.

RHONDA. Who's rootin' for us?

DAVE. Everybody! East and Gayle and Lendall and Randy and Chad —

RHONDA. Well, they never told me that, that they're "rootin'" fer us —

DAVE. Well, that's 'cause you're a little hung up, there, Rhonda! *(Beat. He has scraped something deep inside Rhonda.)* Just — … I'm sorry if I made you mad. I don't know what I did wrong. I just gave you a kiss. I mean, just … why not give me one back? It's the polite thing to do, you know, get a kiss/give a kiss, very fair. Just … give me a kiss, Rhonda. *(Beat.)*

RHONDA. I don't know how.

DAVE. What do you mean?

RHONDA. I don't know how. I've never done it before.

DAVE. You never … kissed?

RHONDA. I won arm wrestling at every Winter Carnival from fifth grade on and I work in plywood at Bushey's Lumber Mill, and that's not what most men wanna … want.

DAVE. Oh, now, where do you get that?

RHONDA. From *everybody.*

DAVE. Well then … you got it wrong, Rhonda, 'cause, I gotta tell ya, there's a lotta guys that take good long looks at you! *(Beat.)* Holy Cow: So, you never — . You never … have *[had … relations]* …?

RHONDA. No.

DAVE. Well, gosh. I think that's kinda neat. *(Beat.)* You know what?, do me a favor: Try givin' me a kiss and see what happens. And I'm not gonna make fun of you or nothin' bad like that, I promise …

RHONDA. No … No … Let's do the *(Going back to her chair so she can work on the painting.)* this: Is it apples? Cherries? Big open-faced strawberry rhubarb pie — *(Dave kisses Rhonda. For a while. Eventually, Dave gently breaks the kiss, checks on her. She's okay. Looks like she liked it this time. The painting should be in Rhonda's eye line during/after this kiss, because now … she's finally going to be able to see what Dave has painted for her.)* Oh, Dave … I see it! It's a — . I see it. It's — … *(Getting up from her chair and getting the painting — so the audience can't see it.)* It's nice. That's really nice. It's good. You're *good* at this! *(She clutches the painting to her chest — the audience still can't see it.)*

DAVE. Yeah?

RHONDA. Yeah.

DAVE. *(Kisses Rhonda. The painting is squished between their bodies — the audience still can't see what it is!)* And *you* are very good at *this* …

RHONDA. *(Kisses Dave hard — and she really is very good at it, which catches Dave by surprise.)* I thought it'd be hard! *(She kisses him again, fast and hard.)* And it's not!!! *(She kisses him again, fast and hard.)* At all … *(The painting — now an afterthought — ends up facing upstage in Rhonda's chair; the audience still hasn't seen it.)* And I feel like I wanna do it for a long time, but I also feel like I wanna do somethin' else … next … *(Rhonda is just about jumping out of her skin, dying to know what's next.)* But I don't know what that is.

DAVE. I do. *(Music. The anticipation is killing them both. But finally, Dave musters his courage, and shows Rhonda what they might wanna do next … by gently unzipping her Polaris snowmobile jacket and taking it off. He then unzips his Arctic Cat snowmobile jacket — with her help! — and takes it off. Then he takes off his boots; indicates that Rhonda should do the same. And Rhonda does. Dave then takes off his snowmobile pants. Rhonda takes off hers. And then Rhonda and Dave start to take off layer after layer after layer [the more layers the better — and funnier!] of snowmobile/winter clothes, which they do more and more rapidly and with more and more intention until it's a bit of a frenzy, and we end up with two people from Northern Maine facing each other wearing only their long johns … and a great big pile of winter clothes on the ground between them. Beat. They're dying for each other!)* You wanna know what comes next-next?

RHONDA. Yeah.

DAVE. Why don't we go inside … and I'll show you …

RHONDA. Well, how long is it gonna take?

DAVE. Well … it could take all night. Maybe longer …

RHONDA. Well, wait! *(Music fades down.)* We're workin' tomorrow, first shift.

DAVE. Says who? *(Beat. He shrugs — he has an idea.)*

RHONDA. *(Gets what he's saying!)* You mean call in? We're callin' in?!? *(Music fades back up. This is a very exciting idea — because these people never call in!)* We're callin' in!!! *(Very excited!)* We're callin' Chad!!! *(Very, very excited!)* 'Cause you and me, we're not working first shift or *any* shift tomorrow. *(Still very, very excited, Rhonda starts to exit into the house; stops — and this is Rhonda's own special brand of seduction:)* You get yourself *inside*, here, Mister Arctic Cat-Man and you show me what's *next!* (She raucously exits into the house. Beat. Dave is amazed — a bit stunned. The way this has panned out is far beyond his wildest dreams! And it's because of his painting, which he now picks up — still so the audience can't see it — and has a moment with. He looks at it, clutches it to himself, and gives thanks! He is interrupted by Rhonda:)* DAVE!! *(Snapped out of his reverie, Dave exits, to live out this dream. As he does so, he quickly, casually, unstage-ily leaves the painting behind in such a way that it finds itself sitting on the chair's arms, propped up against the chair's back, so that the audience can finally see that it is a painting of … a HEART. Just a big, red HEART. Lights fade. The HEART remains lit. Music up. End of "Seeing the Thing." After the lights have faded on "Seeing the Thing," the painting of the heart remains brilliantly lit. It seems to glow brighter for a while, and then, suddenly — music ends/blackout/transitional aurora, and we move to the …*

EPILOGUE

Music. Lights up to reveal Pete, who is still exactly where we left him in the "Interlogue": sitting on his bench, looking off left to where Ginette exited. His snowball is still sitting next to him. Pete gets up, taking his snowball with him, and goes toward where Ginette exited to see if he can see her. And then ... there's a wonderful little swell in the music as ... Ginette slowly — maybe a little wearily — enters from the other side of the stage, stage right! It starts to SNOW! Pete senses Ginette; turns to her; starts towards her — but stops and, first, nonverbally asks, using the snowball, if she's been all the way around the world ... and she nods, "Yes," because she has! She's been all the way around the world and she's back — and she's "close" again. Pete tosses his snowball behind him, and Ginette and Pete run to each other and hug. They go to the bench, sit, and, on the last chord of the music, resume looking at the stars. The northern lights appear. Music ends. Lights fade to black.

End of Play

PROPERTY LIST

PROLOGUE/INTERLOGUE/EPILOGUE:
Snowball

Scene 1, HER HEART:
Small brown paper grocery bag, filled with 19 small slate pieces
Maine travel brochure

Scene 2, SAD AND GLAD:
2 bottles of Budweiser
Tray for waitress

Scene 3, THIS HURTS:
Man's shirt, ironing board, iron, laundry basket filled with folded
    laundry
Composition books, pencil

Scene 4, GETTING IT BACK:
Red bags filled with foam or stuffing
Small pouch with ring box (and ring) inside

Scene 5, THEY FELL:
2 cans of Natural Lite beer

Scene 6, WHERE IT WENT:
Men's hockey skates, women's figure skates, winter shoe

Scene 7, STORY OF HOPE:
Purse, suitcase

Scene 8, SEEING THE THING:
Wrapped painting

SOUND EFFECTS

Scene 1, HER HEART:
Screen door opens, slams

Scene 2, SAD AND GLAD:
Bar activity, bachelorette party noise

Scene 4, GETTING IT BACK:
Pounding on door, door opening and closing, car doors opening
and closing

Scene 6, WHERE IT WENT:
Car door opening and closing, car starting, leaving

Scene 7, STORY OF HOPE.
Car approaching, idling and leaving, doorbell, fancy-shoed
footsteps in snow, door opening and closing

Scene 8, SEEING THE THING:
Snowmobiles approach, park

NOTES FOR DIRECTORS

On the "Prologue," "Interlogue," and "Epilogue:"

Don't be afraid to take *time* in these sequences. Honor the quiet moments — throughout the play.

In the "Prologue," please honor that long opening beat. When Ginette leaves, please follow the stage directions closely. They are the actors' "lines."

If done properly, the "Epilogue" can lift *Almost, Maine* one dramatic notch higher than the end of Scene Eight ("Seeing the Thing"). Ginette's return should be huge and rousing and epic and glorious. She has walked all the way around the world in an instant ... and that is miraculous.

Please rehearse these sequences properly. Don't underestimate them.

On structure:

Almost, Maine is unique in that it is comprised of nine complete tales, each of which begins, climaxes, and ends. Audiences are asked to invest and reinvest in new stories and new characters throughout the play. Therefore, the transitions between scenes will be crucial. They'll serve as necessary little rest periods — but rest periods during which the audience must not be allowed to disengage! So ... be creative with them. Enjoy them. But do so efficiently. Keep them as short as possible. This can best be accomplished when there isn't much stuff to clear/set up between scenes. A couple of ideas: In the Off-Broadway production of the play, Gabe Barre created "parka people" to clear and reset the stage during the transitions. And ... I wonder if it might be interesting to try using title cards inside the transitions to introduce/end each scene.

Keep in mind that each scene in *Almost, Maine* is its own unique emotional nut to crack. Serve each one well and individually. If the parts are well done, the sum of the parts will be well done and effective, and the natural progression of the scenes will fuel the overall arc of the play.

Please note that the endings of the individual scenes in *Almost, Maine* are crucial. They're not easy, happy endings. They're not endings at all, actually. They are complex, fragile, and sometimes awful *suspensions*, fraught with uncertainty. In each scene, the lights should fade on that suspended uncertainty. I do think that, at the close of each scene in the play, the residents of Almost are *about* to experience joy. Great joy. But not just yet — not in what I've written. In what I've written, the lights fade on the moment of change. And change is hard and confusing and uncertain. So don't cheat. Don't skip those uncertain, scary, trepidatious feelings. Don't go straight to the joy. The real, unmitigated joy happens *after* the blackout. What the folks of Almost (and what the audience) experience at the end of these scenes is that moment just *before* the joy! It's there, bubbling under the surface, and I definitely think there's room for a *hint* of the joy to come. But — going *straight* to joy at the end of each scene is the corny, easy way to do this play. And nothing in this play should be corny. Or easy. Because love isn't easy in any of these scenes. Especially in Scenes Six and Seven ("Where It Went" and "Story of Hope"). If you manage to keep the endings suspended, and keep the audience *almost* happy, *wanting* for resolution and catharsis until the very end of the last scene of the play, you'll have done your job perfectly! Only at the end of "Seeing the Thing" — when the clothes come off! — does the audience get a true, cathartic "happy ending." Joy has to be earned, and I think only Rhonda and Dave have earned it. All of the other folks in this play have to wade through fear or sadness or pain before they get the joy! Make the audience wade with them! The "*almost*-happiness" of Scenes One through Five and the bittersweetness — heck, *bitterness* — of Scenes Six and Seven will make the end of Scene Eight wonderfully cathartic, and deliriously joyful. (And, yes, the last scene of Act One — "Getting It Back" — has a pretty happy ending, but that whole scene is a fight — the consequences of which must be dealt with. And, yes, the "Epilogue" has a happy ending, too! But the joy there has been earned, because the "Prologue" ends in the utter uncertainty of a quiet, gentle disaster ... and Ginette's epic journey makes all well.)

On language:

I call the dialogue in *Almost, Maine* "quietly heightened." It's not particularly poetic. It's true to the way people talk. So please encourage your actors to talk the way people talk, not the way actors talk. And — although I don't think I've written poetic language — I think I *have* written poetic *situations*. This is the kind of poetry I like: poetry that is well disguised; poetry that sneaks up on an audience; poetry that surprises. Unexpected poetry gets people where it counts — in their hearts and souls.

General note:

I think *Almost, Maine* can best be described as a midwinter night's dream. Or as a romance. A really funny, really sad romance. It's been fun for me to watch audiences take in the first few productions of *Almost, Maine*, because they think they're watching a simple, realistic little comedy ... and then, all of a sudden, they're not. They're watching something that isn't simple or real or comic at all. Nothing is what it seems. And this surprises people. And it's wonderful to watch people get surprised. People laugh when they're surprised. They gasp. They make strange sounds. This should be your goal as you direct the play: Make the audience make noise. Make them laugh and gasp and utter. Make them desperately wonder if what seems to be unfolding before their very eyes ... is actually unfolding before their very eyes! Keep them guessing. Stay ahead of them. Don't give them what they expect. Don't telegraph. Keep the surprises alive. If you don't succeed in this — then *Almost, Maine* will languish in corny sentimentality. And it will be bad. Because this play is *almost* bad. It toes the line. Don't let it be bad. Make it good. Great, even.

NOTES FOR DESIGNERS

On creating place:

Almost, Maine is a quiet, remote, sometimes lonely place. It is empty. The people of Almost live uncluttered lives. Keep this in mind as you decide how much stuff you need to define the different locales of *Almost, Maine*. I think the less stuff the better. The bleaker the better — it will play nicely against the sweetness and (presumed) sentimentality of the play.

As you think about creating the "town" of Almost, Maine, please consider visiting www.crownofmaine.com for terrific photos of Northern Maine. Look for links to photos by Ken Lamb and Paul Cyr.

And — here's something that I'm not sure anyone can do anything about, but it's always been on my mind. When people think of Maine, they think of lobster and the ocean. Almost, Maine is nowhere near the ocean. It's like Minnesota — but the people aren't Midwestern. I've tried to make this clear as subtly as possible in the text — but it takes a lot more to break down a common misconception than a passing mention! *Anything* you can do to help people understand what and where this very special place is would be very much appreciated. (A map in the program might help with the "where" part.)

On creating the northern lights/"aurora moments:"

The northern lights are not complex and extravagant. They're clean lines of light — like ribbons or curtains. They can be white, yellow, green, red, blue, or purple, depending on what gas is being ionized. The most common color combinations are green and red. I believe ionized lower atmosphere oxygen makes the green color; ionized upper atmosphere oxygen makes the red color. Red is rarer. But better for this play, I think. I've seen yellow, white, and green most frequently; red, occasionally; blue, once (most beautiful thing I've ever seen); purple, never. Whenever I've seen the northern lights, I've felt like they're alive. They *move*. And they are soundless — but when they appear, it feels like there's a humming in the air. This humming is sensed more than heard. Light and some sort of subtle sound might work to help capture the mystery/enhance the creation of the northern lights.

On costumes:

The people of Almost, Maine don't wear funny clothes and funny hats. Keep the clothes simple and functional. Functional winter clothes … are actually quite funny.

On music:

Interstitial music will play a big part in *Almost, Maine*. Julian Fleisher's music is available, and was written for the play, so I *strongly* encourage its use! If you do use other music, try not to use music with lyrics. I think instrumental folk music is the way to go — stuff that features more guitar, hammer dulcimer, harmonica, fiddle, etc. Music with lyrics tends to provide an analysis of what has just happened — and I really want the stories to speak for themselves. Let the scenes be the songs.

NOTES FOR ACTORS

On punctuation:

I've addressed the // and > symbols in the "Notes" section at the beginning of this volume. I just wanted to remind you that the overlaps are very specific and difficult. Please figure them out — accurately! Please remember that > just means GO! And don't stop for the other character's line! Drive through to the end of the sentence or thought! Because pace is key to this play; keeping your lines of thought active is key to this play; and noting when the characters are actually listening to each other is key to this play. Often you'll be playing people who *aren't* listening to each other. Explore that — the non-listening that happens when people are thinking, or are too busy talking. I think the big epiphanies come when people actually listen to and hear each other — and I think epiphanies are rather rare.

Some other punctuation notes:

Sometimes you'll see commas after exclamation points or question marks:

RHONDA: Hey-hey-hey!, okay, okay!!

This is simply to encourage pace and keep things moving. Push through to the landing place — which is, in this case, the double exclamation point.

Sometimes you'll see lines in brackets like these [ ]. They shouldn't be spoken. They're just guides.

A dash (—) at the end of a line means that the next speaker cuts off the current speaker.

A dash followed by a period (—.) or a dash followed by an ellipsis (— ...) at the end of a line means that the person speaking cuts him/herself off with thought. The next character to speak *does not* do the cutting off.

An ellipsis (...) at the end of a line means that the thought trails off.

A dash followed by a period (—.) or a dash followed by an ellipsis (— ...) inside a line means that the person speaking cuts him/herself off with thought before moving on.

On language:

Please honor the beats — the quiet moments — in *Almost, Maine*. And make sure they are full and electric. This play must never feel ... slow. There's a buoyancy to the material. A lightness. And I think it's in the language. Find where the words come tumbling out of the characters' mouths. Find where the words don't come so easy — where the quiet moments are. Much is "said" in those quiet moments. The play must continue to move forward inside those quiet moments.

Please note that the characters from out of town (Glory and Hope) talk more, and faster, than the people of Almost — they have most of the play's monologues. They use words to cover, to protect themselves, to push people away.

On dialect:

Northern Mainers don't really have a distinctive dialect, though r's are pretty pronounced. Words like "sorry" or "forest" or "tomorrow" are pronounced "SORE-ee," "FORE-est," and "to-MORE-ow." The "or" sound is the key. That's about all I'd do with dialect — because the Maine dialect most people know of is a coastal thing, and Almost, Maine is a couple hundred miles from the ocean. It's not "Down East," so please don't do "Down East" Maine. Please. It's not who these people are. Do not think "lobstah" or "A-yuh." Just talk. And hit your r's a little harder than you normally might.

On the "Prologue," "Interlogue," and "Epilogue:"

Please follow the stage directions very closely at the end of the "Prologue," and in the "Interlogue" and "Epilogue." They are your "lines."

On the ironing board hits in "This Hurts" (Scene Four):

The ironing board hits should be as real as can be, as surprising as can be, and as simple as can be. Marvalyn should always "operate" the ironing board with both hands. The key to hitting Steve is in the pivot. Marvalyn should choose a point upon which to pivot as she simply turns to go and put the ironing board away. The momentum of her turn will generate enough speed to make for a pretty great wallop of Steve. Steve might want to see if there's any way to let a hand take the brunt of/amplify each hit.

On characterization:

Your job as an actor in these plays is to tell the stories. You're a storyteller. Don't worry too much about being a chameleon. Don't create caricatures. Sure, you want to create distinct characters — but trust the stories to do a lot of that work for you. Tell the stories, and allow the characters to come to life. This doesn't mean be lazy. It doesn't mean don't be outrageous. It doesn't mean don't be creative. It doesn't mean do nothing or be boring. It just means … construct truthfully!

And, finally (and this is in the previous notes section, but I can't stress its importance enough), the people of Almost, Maine are not simpletons. They are not hicks or rednecks (though Randy and Chad and Rhonda come pretty close). They are not quaint, quirky eccentrics. They don't wear funny clothes and funny hats. They don't have funny Maine accents. They are not "Down Easters." They are not fishermen or lobstermen. They don't wear galoshes and rain hats. They don't say, "Ayuh."

The people of Almost, Maine are ordinary people. (It's their *situations* that are odd and extraordinary.) They work hard for a living. They are extremely dignified. They are honest and true. They are not cynical. They are not sarcastic. They are not glib. But this does not mean that they're dumb. They're very smart. They just take time to wonder about things. What makes these people so special is their guilelessness. We see them think and figure things out. When they speak, they do so simply, honestly, truly, and from the heart. They are never precious about what they say or do.

Please keep in mind that "cute" will kill this play. *Almost, Maine* is inherently pretty sweet. There is no need to sentimentalize the material. Just … let it be what it is — a play about real people who are really, truly, honestly dealing with the toughest thing there is to deal with in life: love.

My advice: Don't forget how much the people of *Almost, Maine* are hurting. Honor the ache, play the pain (keep most of it covered), and don't forget that *Almost, Maine* is a comedy. Sadness and pain are the funniest things in the world.

Things you should know about Maine and Almost, Maine:

Maine is the easternmost and northeasternmost state in the United States.

Maine has 611 miles of international border with Canada, more than any other state except Alaska and Michigan.

Maine is the only state in the country that's attached to only one other state.

Maine is about the same size as the rest of the New England states combined, with a total area of about 35,400 square miles. The other New England states (Vermont, New Hampshire, Massachusetts, Connecticut, and Rhode Island) have a total area of about 36,600 square miles. Although it comprises almost half of New England's total land area, Maine contains only 9% of the region's population.

With 1.3 million residents, Maine is the most sparsely populated state east of the Mississippi River. It has 40 people per square mile. (Consider this: Vermont — *Vermont* — has 65 people per square mile; Massachusetts has 810; New Jersey: 1,100.)

Maine's largest city is Portland, pop. 65,000. (Consider this: Greenwich, CT has 61,000 residents.) Only Vermont, West Virginia, and Wyoming have smaller "largest cities."

Maine's unorganized territories make up more than half of the state's total land area.

Maine is more forested than any other state in the country. It is 90% woods.

Maine has more moose per square mile than any other state.

Maine contains the northern terminus of the Appalachian

Trail: Mt. Katahdin in Central Maine.

Almost, Maine would be located 120 miles north of Mt. Katahdin, in the heart of Aroostook County. Aroostook is the largest county east of the Mississippi River, with a land area of 6,700 square miles. It is almost as big as Massachusetts, whose total land area is 7,800 square miles, and it isn't that much smaller than New Hampshire or Vermont, which are about 9,000 square miles each. Aroostook County is considerably larger than Connecticut (4,800 sq. mi.) and Rhode Island (1,045 sq. mi.) put together.

Aroostook County's population is about 72,000, making it one of the most sparsely populated counties east of the Mississippi. (Connecticut and Rhode Island's combined population is 4.5 *million*.) Aroostook has about 11 people per square mile, making it about as densely populated as the Dakotas.

Population: probably about 300.
Median annual household income: probably about $25,000.
Hours of daylight in mid-January: about 9.
Average January temperature: 9 degrees Fahrenheit.
Average annual snowfall: 115 inches. (Appropriate, then, that — as of this printing — one of Maine's Senators is Olympia Snowe. Senator Snowe. For real.)

Thank you for reading. Thank you for doing my play. Thanks for believing in a place like Almost, Maine!

—John Cariani

CANADA
(NEW BRUNSWICK)

Almost

ME

CANADA
(QUEBEC)

VT

NH

NY

ATLANTIC
OCEAN

MA

RI

CT